Elementary Principal's Model Letter Kit

With Reproducible Illustrations to Enhance Your Messages!

Elementary Principal's Model Letter Kit

With Reproducible Illustrations to Enhance Your Messages!

Fred B. Chernow and Carol Chernow

Illustrated by Carolyn Quinton Oesman

PARKER PUBLISHING COMPANY
West Nyack, New York 10995

Library of Congress Cataloging-in-Publication Data

Chernow, Fred B.
  Elementary principal's model letter kit.

  Includes index.
  1. Elementary school administration—United States.
2. Form letters.   3. Schools—United States—Records
and correspondence—Forms.   I. Chernow, Carol,
II. Title.
LB2822.5.C43 1988   372.12'00973   87-32799
ISBN 0-13-259441-2

ISBN 0-13-259441-2

PARKER PUBLISHING COMPANY
BUSINESS & PROFESSIONAL DIVISION
A division of Simon & Schuster
West Nyack, New York 10995

Printed in the United States of America

About the Authors

Fred B. Chernow is the principal of an elementary school on Staten Island, New York. He has conducted in-service courses for teachers as well as seminars for business and professional leaders in letter writing and communication skills. He is an adjunct professor at St. John's University.

Carol Chernow is an English teacher at a large, multiethnic intermediate school. She has taught elementary grades in Maryland and communication skills to adults for the Federal government.

Both of the Chernows have had several books published by Prentice-Hall, including their best-selling *Classroom Discipline and Control*.

About This Kit

Have you ever wished you could write letters and memos that would persuade people to do what you want—to do what is best for your students and your school? Have you ever wanted to spend less time writing letters that sometimes go unread? The *Elementary Principal's Model Letter Kit* offers you a collection of over 300 model letters and memos that cover virtually every school situation you may face. With it, the know-how you need is right in the palm of your hand.

The letters and memos in the *Kit* are mainly printed one to a page so you can easily adapt them to suit your particular situation. These models help you seize new opportunities to build your school's and its principal's reputation.

Many letters appear with lively artwork to enhance their message. And, with just a photocopier, a pair of scissors and a roll of tape, the artwork from one letter can easily be mixed and matched with a letter from another page. This book will help you upgrade the letters you frequently write and also give you ideas for new situations where the right letter will improve your standing with the following school communities:

- PARENTS: Among the 113 letters in Section 1, you will pick up pointers on writing policy statements on homework, warning letters on failing grades, thank-you letters of various types, and even sample letters in Spanish and English on head lice.

- PUPILS: Section 2's collection ranges from academic contracts to yearbook messages. You will have at your fingertips a selection of models dealing with dress codes, honor rolls, bus safety, a summer reading list, vandalism, and other current topics.

- TEACHERS: In Section 3, you will find over 70 letters both to individuals and the entire faculty. The subjects include general statements, curriculum, lesson plans, classroom appearance, substitute teachers, evaluation, referral of students, and personal letters of recommendation and sympathy.

- OTHER STAFF MEMBERS: Section 4 focuses on ways to communicate with the custodian, school secretary, guidance counselor, paraprofessionals, nurse, and others. These model letters and memos will improve your techniques of administration and delegation.

- SPECIAL EVENTS: Section 5 enhances your ability to provide and publicize special events in your school. Covered in this section are all kinds of contests, school fairs, award programs, and a collection of special events for each month of the school year.

- THE COMMUNITY: Section 6 helps you improve your degree of community involvement. These models run the gamut from alumni to volunteers, and cover some of the toughest letter-writing situations with ease and fluency.

Using the proven and provocative ideas in *Elementary Principal's Model Letter Kit,* you will be able to:

- improve the image of your school
- raise the level of staff morale
- encourage greater parent support
- involve students in cooperative efforts
- increase your sense of job satisfaction
- save hours of your valuable time

Hundreds of successful school administrators have developed and refined these letters in their schools, thereby opening up their channels of communication and winning the support and confidence of others. You will find countless timesaving, problem-solving techniques and tips which you will want to put to use immediately in your elementary school.

You will quickly learn how to use:

- strategies for spreading the word about the positive things happening at your school
- suggestions for notifying teachers and parents about upcoming events and winning their support and assistance
- hints for saying what you mean in a way that will get immediate attention and cheerful compliance
- tips on using supercharged words, phrases, and topics to improve your stature in your school community
- examples of letters, memos, press releases, conference notes, and other communications guaranteed to build bridges between you and the people you supervise and relate to *every day*
- devices for producing amazing results when you want to inform or convince others

In addition, in this *Kit* you will discover answers to six questions that stymie so many good principals:

1. How can I get the students in my school to follow rules and regulations?
2. How can I gain the support of my faculty when they do not always read the notices I send them?
3. How can I reach parents who are so burdened with daily problems that they have little time for school newsletters or announcements?
4. How can I get the custodial, secretarial, lunch, and security staff to feel they are part of the school team—and that I am the captain?

5. How can I increase attendance at school events and make the community my partner in education?

6. How can I use letters to foster agreement instead of opposition and cooperation instead of resistance?

You will be amazed at the turnabout in your effectiveness as a communicator and as a leader when using these models. At last, you will know how to get your ideas across to others, and you will be able to reach hundreds with just the flick of the "start" button on your copy machine.

The one-letter-per-page format will give you immediate feedback as to how the letter will look over your signature. By copying the single page and making minor changes on it, you can then hand your typist one piece of paper with all or most of the copy already laid out. When appropriate, you can use or eliminate the sample art as you wish, because these are letters you can use *every day*.

Elementary Principal's Model Letter Kit is a practical timesaver that will help you send intelligent and informative messages to the wider community, as well as to your students and staff. Using this collection of letters and memos will help prevent communication problems and foster an improved image for even the most experienced school leader.

Fred B. Chernow
Carol Chernow

Contents

SECTION 1
Letters to Parents • 1

SECTION 2
Letters to Students • 119

SECTION 3
Letters to Teachers • 163

SECTION 4
Letters to Staff Members • 249

SECTION 5
Letters for Special Events • 281

SECTION 6
Letters to the Community • 319

Elementary Principal's Model Letter Kit

With Reproducible Illustrations to Enhance Your Messages!

Letters
to
Parents

Letter 1–1: ABSENCE

April 11, 19XX
RE: Kevin McGill
Class: 4B

Dear Mr. and Mrs. McGill:

    Your child, Kevin, was absent from school on Wednesday, April 9, 19XX. It is the policy of the Board of Education to have every absence accounted for by receiving a note of excuse from the parent or guardian.

    Please indicate below the reason for this absence and return it promptly to the classroom teacher, Mr. Corbett.

    Prompt and regular attendance is necessary for successful school work.

    Thank you for your cooperation.

Sincerely,

_____

V. DiAngelo, Principal

--------------------------- Please tear off and return to school ---------------------------

Dear _____,

    My child, _____, was absent on _____ because

_____

_____

Child's Name: _____ Class: _____

_____

Parent's Signature

Letter 1–2: ATTENDANCE

Date: November 3, 19XX

Dear Parents:

In keeping with our efforts to do the utmost for all of the children, I once again ask for your cooperation and assistance in the matter of pupil attendance.

I have stressed many times the importance of regular attendance in order that each child receive the maximum benefits from regular daily sequential instruction.

We urge all our parents to assist us in our goals, which we all realize are necessary to give our children every opportunity to benefit from regular attendance at school.

Of course, children cannot attend when they are ill, but there are few other reason for nonattendance. However, it is better for a child to come to school late or for part of the day than to miss the entire day.

I know I have the cooperation of all our parents.

Sincerely,

_____

V. DiAngelo, Principal

Letter 1-3: ATTENDANCE

Date: December 16, 19XX

Dear Parents:

Once again I must ask your cooperation in the matter of pupil attendance. Our teachers are most anxious to have all the children benefit from the lessons they have prepared. It is difficult to have pupils make up work when they are absent frequently.

We urge all parents to keep pupils at home only when it is necessary for health reasons. While we do not want pupils to attend school when they are ill, we do want them to come to school on all other school days.

So far this year, your child _____ has been absent on these dates:

_____

_____

_____

_____

Please check to see that you were aware of these dates. If you have any questions, do not hesitate to call the attendance teacher at 761-1234. Since this letter is going out to all parents whose children were absent 15 or more days, do not be offended by our request that you check the dates of nonattendance. There are some children who are absent without their parents' knowledge.

Sincerely,

_____

V. DiAngelo, Principal

Letter 1–4: NONATTENDANCE

January 15, 19XX
RE: Rebecca Ferguson
Class: 3A

Dear Mr. and Mrs. Ferguson:

The progress of your child in school depends greatly on regular attendance and not missing class time. We need your cooperation and support on this matter. Please respond by returning the reply portion of this letter or call me at 761-5511 as soon as possible.

Reason: _____ Unexcused absence _____ Lateness to school

_____ Excessive absence _____ Late to class _____ Excessive use of bathroom

_____ Other

Comments: _____

_____

Sincerely,

_____

V. DiAngelo, Principal

----------------------------------- Detach and Return -----------------------------------

Reply by Parent re: Nonattendance Letter dated January 15, 19xx:

_____

_____

_____

_____

Parent's Signature: _____ Pupil: _____ Class: _____

Letter 1–5: CONTINUED ATTENDANCE

Date: May 26, 19XX

Dear Parent:

It has been a pleasure having your youngster in our school this past year. We are now making plans for next year and need to know if your child will be in attendance.

1. Do you plan to move out of the district before September?

_____ Yes _____ No

2. Will any of your children be attending a private or parochial school next year instead of this school?

_____ Yes _____ No

If "yes," the name or names of the child(ren):

_____

_____

We must have this information by June 8th and we appreciate your cooperation. Thank you.

Yours truly,

_____

V. DiAngelo, Principal

------------------------------------ Detach and Return ------------------------------------

Dear Principal:

I have received your notice concerning pupil attendance for next year.

_____ My child or children plan to remain at school.

_____ My child or children plan to attend another elementary school. I have listed their name(s) and the name of the other school above.

_____

| Parent's Signature | Child's Class | Date |

Letter 1–6: BEHAVIOR WARNING

October 19, 19XX
RE: Greg Hillier
Class: 6A

Dear Mr. and Mrs. Hillier:

In spite of repeated warnings, your child Greg continues to be disruptive during the Social Studies program. We are being forced to remove him/her from the program until there is a sign of improvement in attitude and behavior.

Please discuss this with your child. As soon as we see some serious attempt by your child to improve, we will be happy to restore all privileges.

Sincerely,

_____

V. DiAngelo, Principal

Letter 1–7: IMPROVED BEHAVIOR

December 4, 19XX
RE: Lonnie Morrison
Class: 2C

Dear Mr. and Mrs. Morrison:

Because of your interest in Lonnie's behavior, I want to report to you some improvement has been noticed. His teacher, Ms. Van Houten, has reported the following:

_____

_____

_____

At present, there is still room for improvement. Especially when

_____

_____

_____

Please write down your comments and have Lonnie return this letter to me at school. By communicating with us in this way, I am certain that Lonnie's behavior will continue to improve.

Sincerely,

_____

V. DiAngelo, Principal

Letter 1–8: BUDGET

Date: January 25, 19XX

TO: Parents
RE: Budget Crunch

Because of the recent budget cuts, one of the items eliminated was funds for buses for after-school and special activities. This will result in a loss of field trips and participation in after-school activities.

We need your help in keeping these cuts from destroying these extracurricular activities for our pupils. Parent volunteers willing to car pool and provide the necessary transportation are our hope. Can we count on you to join other parents in providing the needed car service?

With your help as a volunteer chauffeur, our clubs and activities will continue to flourish, our teams will still be able to practice and play, and our special events will take place.

Please fill out the attached stub and return it to school with your son or daughter.

Thank you for your cooperation.

Sincerely,

_____

V. DiAngelo, Principal

Dear Principal:

I read your letter dated January 25 regarding the cuts in bus service. I will be able to provide help in transporting pupils on these days of the week at these times:

_____

_____

I can be reached at: _____

Parent's Signature:_____Student's Name:_____

Class:_____

Letter 1–9: BUDGET

Date: March 13, 19XX

Dear Parents:

Our school faces a crisis. The strong educational program that we have taken pride in is on the verge of collapse. What we have built slowly and steadily is being wiped out by the stroke of a red pencil.

Our tentative allocation will cause a drastic reduction in services. Please be aware that this allocation is <u>more</u> than we may receive if we are funded at the so-called "crisis budget" level.

Based on the tentative allocation, this reduction will eliminate:

1. One Grade 5 class
2. One Grade 4 class
3. The Music Cluster position
4. The School Band
5. Our Guidance Counselor

Other ramifications include:

1. Increased class size
2. Less supportive help
3. Loss of special programs

I plead with all parents to contact their legislators and indicate the seriousness of the situation. The attached list of addresses will help you contact them promptly.

On behalf of your children, I urge you to write today.

Sincerely,

_____

V. DiAngelo, Principal

Letter 1–10: POOR BUS SERVICE

Dear Mr. McGuire:

Thank you for your letter of March 1, 19XX in which you mention that your child, Raymond, in Class 3A missed the school bus at dismissal time. You point out that the Route Four bus left our school before the scheduled time.

I have checked this matter with Miss Robinson who puts the children on the bus. She says that this has been a problem on a few occasions. I have since taken the matter up with Mr. Delgado, the Supervisor at Pioneer Bus Company. He assures me that this will not happen again. He realizes what a hardship this places on a child's family when they must suddenly make other arrangements to pick their child up at school.

This afternoon I spoke to Raymond and emphasized how important it is for him to report to the bus line promptly at 3:00 P.M. His teacher, Ms. Buckner will be sure he is dismissed on time to make the bus. Most of all, I pointed out to the bus driver the need for him to adhere to the dismissal schedule.

Your comments on the bus service and all other school matters are always most welcome.

Yours truly,

_____

V. DiAngelo, Principal

Letter 1–11: BUS RULES

TO: Parents of Pupils Riding the School Bus
RE: Rules and Regulations

     The "Rules and Regulations for Pupils Riding the School Bus" are quite simple. In order for your child to understand just what is expected, we are enclosing a copy. We suggest that you and your child read these regulations and review them together.

     Both you and your child are being asked to sign this confirmation indicating that you are aware of the rules and the consequences for breaking them. If you want your child to continue to ride the bus, you must return this statement signed by both you and your child.

FOR STUDENT	FOR PARENT
I have read and understand the "Rules and Regulations for Pupils Riding the School Bus," and I agree to follow these rules at all times.	I have read and understand the "Rules and Regulations for Pupils Riding the School Bus," and agree to assume full responsibility for child's behavior on the bus.

_____

Student's Signature

_____

Parent's Signature

_____ _____

Class   Date

_____

Date

Letter 1–12: BEHAVIOR ON THE BUS

October 15, 19XX
RE: Rudy Garcia
Class: 4B

Dear Mr. and Mrs. Garcia:

The driver of Bus #155, Ms. Compton, has reported your child for unsafe conduct on the bus. We are concerned for the safety of your child as well as the safety of all the other children. I am sure you share our concern.

Please speak with your child regarding proper conduct on the school bus. If there is no improvement, your child will be deprived of the privilege of riding the bus.

One of the specific complaints concerns _____

_____

You may call me about this matter at 761-5511.

Sincerely,

_____
V. DiAngelo, Principal

cc:
Pupil Transportation
Pupil's File

I have read this letter on Bus Safety.

_____
Parent's Signature

Letter 1–13: LOSS OF BUS PRIVILEGE

Dear Mr. and Mrs. Zimmer:

On April 14, 19XX your son Alexander was disruptive on his school bus. This action was reported to the building principal and was investigated by Mr. Marchetti.

This was not Alexander's first disruptive behavior. He has been warned previously that this conduct would not be tolerated. Mr. Marchetti spoke with you about this problem and warned of a possible withdrawal of bus riding privileges.

Since Alexander has continued his disruptive behavior we must withdraw his school bus riding privileges for a period of one week beginning April 30. This is in accordance with school board policy (a copy of the policy is attached).

WITHDRAWAL OF BUS RIDING PRIVILEGES DOES NOT RELIEVE THE CHILD OR THE PARENTS OF RESPONSIBILITY UNDER THE SCHOOL ATTENDANCE LAWS. The student must continue to attend school. The parents are required to provide their own transportation while the bus privileges are withdrawn.

Sincerely,

_____

V. DiAngelo, Principal

Letter 1-14: LOSS OF BUS PRIVILEGE

February 5, 19XX
RE: Lynn Chan
Class: 3B

Dear Mr. and Mrs. Chan:

Again on February 4, 19XX your daughter was reported as being disruptive on the school bus by Mr. Timmons, the bus driver. This was investigated by Mr. Marchetti from our school staff.

As you know from our earlier conversations, this was not Lynn's first incident on the bus. She was warned by the teacher on duty and by me that this kind of misbehavior would not be tolerated. I spoke to you last time about the possibility of withdrawal of bus-riding privileges.

We are taking away this privilege for a period of five school days beginning February 8. This is in accordance with school board policy (a copy of which is attached).

Withdrawal of bus riding privileges does not relieve the child or the parents of responsibility under the school attendance laws. The pupil must continue to attend school with the parents providing transportation.

If you have any questions, please call me at 761-5511.

Sincerely,

_____

V. DiAngelo, Principal

Letter 1–15: CHANGE OF CLASS

November 9, 19XX

Dear Mr. and Mrs. Nelson:

I have your letter dated November 4 in which you request a change of class for your daughter Miriam, who is now in class 4B.

Before placing the pupil in a class, we consider many factors, including: achievement test scores, teacher recommendation, and level of performance in previous grade.

I have checked with Mr. Corbett, your child's present teacher, as well as Mr. Zimmerman, her teacher last year. I have also reviewed Miriam's cumulative record card. Based on this review, I feel that your child's present class placement is the best place for her.

If, however, you feel there is some compelling reason to consider a change of class at this time in the school year, you may call me at 761-5511 for an appointment to explore this matter further.

Sincerely,

_____

V. DiAngelo, Principal

Letter 1–16: CHANGE OF CLASS

December 11, 19XX
RE: Regina Williamson
Class: 2A

Dear Mr. and Mrs. Williamson:

I am writing you in regard to your daughter Regina in Mrs. Hoogerhyde's class. From time to time we reevaluate the progress of our pupils and, when necessary, make changes in their class placement.

After careful consideration, Mrs. Hoogerhyde and I agree that a change to class 2C in the same grade is in order for Regina.

This new class placement will begin on December 15. If you have any questions, please feel free to call either Mrs. Perez, the Guidance Counselor, or me at 761-5511.

Sincerely,

_____

V. DiAngelo, Principal

Letter 1–17: REQUEST FOR CLARIFICATION

Dear Mrs. Moore:

Thank you for your inquiry about the manner in which we handle cheating at P.S. 54.

Teachers know that this happens on occasion and we recognize that it is not a good thing. We believe that cheating should not be permitted or encouraged for a number of reasons, among them the possibility that this can lead to unfavorable character development.

For that reason we have a clear policy covering cheating in class. We explain this to the children in general terms in the beginning of the school year and I go over it in some detail with any child who does cheat. The intent, of course, is to help the child understand the possible harm he does to himself by cheating.

A copy of my policy on this matter is enclosed for your convenience.

If you would like to discuss this with me further, please call the school office (761-5511) to make an appointment.

Sincerely,

_____

V. DiAngelo, Principal

Letter 1–18: CONDUCT

November 5, 19XX
RE: Cecilia Moore
Class: 1A

Dear Mr. and Mrs. Moore:

A good attitude in school is the key to academic and personal success. This year we plan some exciting learning experiences including trips, independent study, library visits, and guest speakers. Our plans are wasted unless each child shows self-control. I need your cooperation in helping Cecilia to exercise good conduct in school.

Every Friday he/she will bring home a dated and signed Conduct Slip. If it has "very good" on it, he/she has excelled in self-control and no slips will be sent home until further notice. "Good" means a positive effort was made by your child. "Improvement needed" means a definite lack of self-control. The last mark, "Unsatisfactory," shows complete disregard for class rules and I will ask that you write a response on the back of the slip.

Enclosed is the first conduct slip. Please sign it and have Cecilia return it on Monday. Your cooperation is appreciated. You can reach me at school by calling 761-5511.

Sincerely yours,

_____

V. DiAngelo, Principal

Letter 1–19: CONDUCT

November 24, 19XX
RE: Gary Paulsen
Class: 4A

Dear Mr. and Mrs. Paulsen:

This letter is written to inform you that your child Gary will receive a conduct mark that is less than satisfactory for the current marking period unless there is sufficient improvement in class behavior.

Since the pupil's own progress as well as the rights of others to an uninterrupted education are affected by repeated misconduct, it is the policy of the school to deny all Honors Awards to pupils who receive a conduct mark of less than satisfactory. Promotion at the end of the school year may be denied for serious, uncorrected misconduct.

I will be happy to meet with you in person or by telephone during school hours so that we may plan together for your child's improvement. If you wish such a meeting, please call the school at 761-5511.

Sincerely,

_____

V. DiAngelo, Principal

Letter 1–20: PARENT-TEACHER CONFERENCES

November 16, 19XX

Dear Parents:

Next Tuesday afternoon our school will be holding parent-teacher interviews. In order to make your conference a profitable one, we would like to suggest some things you may want to ask about and some things you may want to tell the teacher.

You may want to ask the teacher:

1. Does my child participate in classroom activities?
2. Does he/she join in discussions or make suggestions?
3. Does my child show self-control in school situations?
4. How does my child get along with the other children?
5. Does he/she relate well to the teacher and other adults?
6. Can my child handle the learning materials of the grade (textbooks, reference books, science materials, gym equipment)?
7. Does he/she seem to enjoy reading during his/her spare time?
8. Is his/her comprehension suitable to his/her grade level?
9. How does my child read orally? Does he/she know the number facts?
10. Can he/she express his/her thoughts and ideas clearly?
11. How is his/her written communication?
12. Does my child seem happy in school? Is he/she accepted by the other children?

You may want to tell the teacher:

1. Which school activities your child talks about at home.
2. What responsibilities your child handles at home.
3. If anything has happened lately at home that might affect your child's performance at school.
4. Which classmates your child sees at home.
5. What are some of your child's favorite activities outside of school.
6. How you discipline your child at home.
7. What are your child's strengths and weaknesses.

Sharing information about your child with his/her teacher will enable us to provide a learning program that will best meet the needs of your child.

Thank you for your cooperation. Remember—the conference times are between 1:00 PM and 4:00 P.M.

Sincerely,

_____

V. DiAngelo, Principal

Letter 1-21: CONGRATULATIONS

May 27, 19XX

Dear Mr. and Mrs. Harrison,

Congratulations on the outstanding academic achievement of your son Douglas. He has placed among the top five students of his class and has earned an academic award as directed by the School Board.

This award carries great significance in our district. Of our total 7,543 District 3 students this year, only 23 received this honor. Thus, his performance ranks him near the top one percent academically of all students in District 3. I know you are proud of him, and I want you to know that his teachers and other school officials are equally proud.

Please pass along to Douglas our congratulations and gratitude for his accomplishments this past year. We are confident that he will maintain this record in the years ahead.

Sincerely,

_____

V. DiAngelo, Principal

Letter 1–22: CONGRATULATIONS

June 2, 19XX

Dear Mr. and Mrs. Marshall:

It is such a pleasure to be writing you to congratulate you on the achievement of your daughter Elizabeth.

When Elizabeth graduates later this month, she will do so with the honor of having the highest academic average in her eighth grade class. With a graduating class of more than 100 students, this is no small achievement. It is reflective of the hard work, perseverence, and application on the part of your daughter. She is to be congratulated on her efforts.

In many ways her achievement is a tribute to you, her parents. It is obvious that a nurturing, supportive atmosphere in your home was a major force in Elizabeth's achievement. My compliments to you.

It will be my pleasure to greet you at Graduation on June 26.

Yours sincerely,

_____

V. DiAngelo, Principal

Letter 1–23: CONGRATULATIONS

April 21, 19XX

Dear Mr. Rivera:

While looking through last night's newspaper I saw the article and photograph describing your promotion.

I was quite impressed, as was your son no doubt. He is doing well at school. I'm sure your promotion at Leonard Industries will continue to motivate him to do his best.

Enclosed is a copy of the piece in the newspaper. Again, congratulations and best wishes for success in your new position. In your household the month of June is not the only time for "promotion."

Sincerely,

_____

V. DiAngelo, Principal

Letter 1–24: CONGRATULATIONS

May 13, 19XX

Dear Mr. and Mrs. O'Connor:

By now you have received the official notice from Hunts Point High School advising you of your daughter's acceptance into their honors program.

I congratulated Joanna in school today on this accomplishment and want to commend you as well. Hunts Point School accepts very few pupils each year into their honors program. I'm sure they will be very glad that they didn't let a pupil like Joanna get away!

It has been a pleasure having Joanna at our school. Her high academic achievement was exceeded only by her charm and modesty. Encourage her to drop us a line after she has settled in. Again, good luck to both of you.

Sincerely,

_____

V. DiAngelo, Principal

Letter 1–25: CONGRATULATIONS

Dear Mr. and Mrs. Allen:

I have already spoken to your daughter, Judy, and offered her my congratulations upon her election to the P.S. 54 Honor Society. I would like to extend those congratulations to you as well. If ever the word "honor" could be extended to describe an individual, it would be proper and fitting in Judy's case. Her high academic record, as well as her record of care and concern for the good of others, mark her as an individual truly worthy of this distinction. I know you must be justly proud of her as we are at the school.

I look forward to meeting you at the ceremonies later this month. I just wanted you to know how highly we regard your daughter and how pleased we are that she is receiving recognition for her achievement.

Sincerely,

_____

V. DiAngelo, Principal

Letter 1–26: CHOICE OF COURSES

TO: Parents

All eighth graders will soon be asked to make their choices of the academic track they will follow in their high school careers. Each student is asked to choose one of the following:

business curriculum
college preparatory curriculum
general education curriculum
technical education curriculum

The choice made now is difficult to change in succeeding years. Hence we ask that both parents and students give long and serious thought to the selection to be made. The final decision should be based on the student's ability and interests as well as his school record to date.

The enclosed booklet describes each curriculum in detail. Requirements, courses to be taken, and job possibilities for graduates are listed for each curriculum.

The Guidance Office is ready to discuss your child's school work and potential with you. We cannot make the decision as to which curriculum your child should follow: that choice is his or hers—and yours. We can help with facts and explanations and we are prepared to do so. Please call Mrs. Perez for an appointment if you wish to discuss this important choice that your child must make.

Sincerely,

_____

V. DiAngelo, Principal

Letter 1–27: NEW PROGRAM OR CURRICULUM

Dear Parents:

This year our school will try a new plan for the improvement of reading. It is really only new to us. It has been used successfully in other school districts for many years. We are adopting the procedure because it has been successful elsewhere and because we think our children will benefit from it.

The plan is really very simple. All students will be grouped for reading by their actual level of skill regardless of grade assignment. As each student progresses in reading skill, he will be moved to the next level. This means that your child may have several different reading teachers this year but he will remain with me most of the time.

We expect the children to be slightly confused at first by the change. However, we feel that they will quickly begin to like the new method because they will not be bored by material that is too easy or frightened by material that is too hard.

We have planned 36 levels of reading for the entire school. The average child should move from levels 1 through 6 in the first grade, 7 through 12 in the second grade, and so on. We know that children learn at different speeds, but the child who learns more slowly than another does learn just as well. Please bear this in mind if your child does not seem to move rapidly.

Because this is important to me, I enforce strict rules during tests. A student who breaks any of these rules has a private conference with me. I tell him then what he did wrong. I also tell him that he is then in the same position as if he had not taken the test at all. Then I will have to find another way to see what he does or does not know. This could mean another test on the same material given to him after school.

The emphasis is not on punishment but on the fact that we must find another way to learn what he needs to know. This can be annoying to both of us and to his parents.

This information sheet is sent to parents so that we can work together for the best interests of all our children.

Sincerely,

_____

V. DiAngelo, Principal

Letter 1–28: CURRICULUM WORKSHOPS

September 19, 19XX

TO: All Parents

You will have an opportunity to meet your child's teacher on a Wednesday afternoon. This will be a group meeting where you will learn about the curriculum, homework policy, standards of written work, conduct code, etc. This is NOT the time to discuss individual pupils. Evening and afternoon meetings will be devoted to that purpose in November.

Please note these dates on your calendar:
Kindergarten– October 1
Grade One   – October 8
Grade Two   –October 15
Grade Three –October 22
Grade Four   –October 29
Grade Five   –November 5

You will report directly to your child's classroom at 2:15 P.M. While you are with the teacher, the class will be in the Auditorium.

I hope you will make every effort to attend.

Yours truly,

_____
V. DiAngelo, Principal

****

Tear off and return to child's teacher

Dear Teacher:

____I will

____I will not   attend the Grade Curriculum Workshop

on_____ in my child's classroom, as per your note of September 19.

_____   _____
Child's Name   Class   Parent's Signature

Letter 1–29: DENTAL HEALTH

Dear Parents:

    Good dental care is essential to your child's health. For those who cannot afford to go to a private dentist, our Health Department provides free dental care at the Lenox Health Center.

    If you cannot afford private dental care for your child, please return the attached note to your child's teacher, requesting treatment. You will then be contacted by the dental hygienist. She will arrange an appointment for you to come to the clinic with your child to sign the necessary dental forms before treatment can be given.

    You must accompany your child for the first visit. This is a rule of the Lenox Health Center.

Yours truly,

_____

V. DiAngelo, Principal

DETACH AND RETURN TO CHILD'S TEACHER

Dear _____:

    _____ I have received your letter regarding the Lenox Health Center's Dental Clinic. I request that my child receive this free service.

    _____ I prefer to have my child treated by a private dentist. I will make an appointment on my own.

_____

Child's Name   Class   Address

_____

Parent's Signature

Letter 1–30: EXTRACURRICULAR ACTIVITIES

Date: February 4, 19XX

TO: Parents of Pupils Involved

We need your permission for your son/daughter _____ of

Class _____ to take part in the extracurricular activity listed below:

_____ Trip to _____ on _____

_____ Attend Field Day

_____ Participate in team sports, i.e. _____

_____ Serve as _____ Monitor

_____ Serve as school crossing guard

_____ Stay after school for _____

Additional description of activity:

_____

_____

_____

_____

Parent's Signature: _____ Date: _____

Phone Number: _____

Letter 1–31: FAILING GRADE

March 8, 19XX
RE: Tony Dispaltro
Class: 7B

Dear Mr. and Mrs. Dispaltro:

This letter is to let you know that your child, Tony, may receive a failing grade in Science for the current marking period unless there is an improvement in the area(s) of student performance noted as follows:

_____ Handing in Homework

_____ Quality of Homework

_____ Participation in Classwork

_____ Test Marks

_____ Attitude

_____ _____

Comments: _____

_____

_____

I will be happy to meet with you in person or on the telephone so that we can plan for your child's success. Please call me at 761-5511. If you wish to speak to your child's teacher, you can make an appointment by calling that same number.

If you wish, you can write me your comments on the back of this letter and return it to me in a sealed envelope through your child or by mail.

Sincerely,

_____
V. DiAngelo, Principal

Letter 1–32: FAILING GRADE

January 11, 19XX
RE: Carla Sitzman
Class: 5A

Dear Mr. and Mrs. Sitzman:

At the present time, your child Carla is doing unsatisfactory work in the following subjects:

_____

_____

_____

This note is to let you know of the situation so that some steps can be taken to make sure that an improvement takes place. There is still time to prevent a final failing grade. When talking to your child's teacher, Mr. Mistretta, the reason for the

unsatisfactory performance seems to be because of _____

_____

_____

_____

I'm sure you share my concern about this matter. While you and the school seem to be concerned, we must now make sure that Carla shares our concern and does something about it.

Sincerely,

_____

V. DiAngelo, Principal

Parent's reply: _____

_____

I would like a conference. A good time for me to come to school would be _____

_____

_____

Parent's Signature

Letter 1–33: FAILING GRADE

December 29, 19XX
RE: Richard Maxwell
Class: 6C

Dear Mr. and Mrs. Maxwell:

By this time, you have seen your child's second report card. A comparison with his first report card and a talk with his teacher shows that Richie is not doing as well as he is able to do.

If there is no improvement for the rest of the year, he may be held over next year.

Please come to school to talk with Mrs. Kinny, the teacher. Mrs. Perez, our Guidance Counselor, will also be happy to meet with you after you speak to your child's teacher. You may reach her at 761-5924.

Please contact Mrs. Kinny, your child's teacher, to arrange for an appointment as soon as possible. With parent-teacher-child cooperation and significant improvement, Richie can move on to the next grade. If there is no significant improvement, he will have to repeat the grade.

Sincerely,

_____

V. DiAngelo, Principal

Letter 1—34: FAILING GRADE

February 16, 19XX
RE: Carol Teischler
Class: 4B

Dear Mrs. Teischler:

At the present time, in spite of our efforts, your child's work in class indicates that she may have to repeat Grade Four next year. In November we sent home a warning letter to you and had a conference with Carol about her poor work in school.

Please make an appointment with Mr. Corbett, her teacher, to see what you can do to effect sufficient improvement by June to permit her promotion to the next grade.

It is important that you see Carol's teacher very soon so that a plan of action can be worked out.

Sincerely,

_____

V. DiAngelo, Principal

Letter 1–35: FAMILY LIVING

October 10, 19XX

TO: Parents, Grades 1–5
RE: Family Living as Part of the Curriculum

The District Office has mandated Parent Curriculum Workshops. They will provide us with a copy of the District 3 grade curriculum to be handed out only to those parents who attend. We hope you will come to school on the dates below.

This year, Family Living has been added to the printed Guide that parents receive. These are the highlights of the new School Board Policy:

- Family Living will be part of the regular curriculum and not a separate subject.
- Parents will be asked to sign a permission slip.
- Children whose parents do not want them to participate will be sent out of the room.
- I will describe the program at a P.T.A. meeting.

We have planned the Workshops during the month of October. Please note the time schedule below. Students will board the bus or walk home from the Auditorium. They will be dismissed at 2:15 P.M. with coats and books.

Topics for discussion include:

1. Homework policy
2. Class routines
3. Trips planned
4. Special programs
5. Enrichment or remedial activities
6. Extensions of the basic curriculum
7. Long-range projects
8. Standards of conduct and dress

Schedule

Thursday, October 13 . . . . Grade 4–2:15 P.M.
Monday, October 17 . . . . Grade 2–2:15 P.M.
Friday, October 21. . . . . Grade 5–2:15 P.M.
Monday, October 24 . . . . Grade 3–2:15 P.M.
Thursday, October 27 . . . . Grade 1–2:15 P.M.

_____

V. DiAngelo, Principal

Letter 1–36: FAREWELL MESSAGE

June 6, 19XX

Dear Parents of Grade 7 Pupils:

We are pleased to invite you to our Seventh Grade Final Assembly on Friday morning, June 21, 19XX, at 9:30 A.M., in our school auditorium.

This is a joyous occasion for our pupils and a proud one for our teachers who have nurtured these young people through the grades. For this special assembly, we are asking that pupils follow this simple dress code:

Boys: Shirt, tie, no jacket

Girls: Simple summer dress or skirt and blouse; no halters, no shorts, no clogs

Our Guest Speaker will be Carl Greenberg, Chairperson of the Community School Board.

At the conclusion of the Final Assembly, at approximately 11:00 A.M., pupils with guests will be excused for an extended lunch hour.

Congratulations and best wishes!

Sincerely,

_____

V. DiAngelo, Principal

Reminder to Pupils: Attendance at this Assembly is a privilege. Pupils who misbehave
will NOT be allowed to attend.

Letter 1-37: FLAG DAY

June 4, 19XX

Dear Parents,

On Thursday, June 14th, P.S. 54 will again celebrate Flag Day with an outdoor ceremony at 10:30 A.M. in our school yard. Parents and pre-school children are invited to attend this annual school event. In case of rain, the ceremony will take place in the Auditorium for Grades 2, 3, and 4 only.

The Fourth Grade band, led by Miss Adamson, will play march music. Pupils will read patriotic selections, and will sing songs. All our Cub Scouts and Brownies will appear in full uniform and carry pack flags as well as American Flags.

Flags of the thirteen original colonies will also fly. <u>All pupils will be dressed in shades of red, white and blue.</u> Please cooperate by helping your child select from his or her regular school wardrobe, clothes that are red, white and/or blue.

We look forward to having you join us on this festive occasion. You may enter the yard on Davis Avenue side.

Sincerely,

_____

V. DiAngelo, Principal

Letter 1–38: GRADUATION

TO: Parents of our Graduates
FR: V. DiAngelo, Principal
RE: Graduation Procedures
DATE: June 8, 19XX

Thanks to your cooperation, encouragement, and effort, your child will graduate from P.S. 54 on Tuesday evening, June 18. We will hold our sixteenth graduation ceremony at 6:30 P.M. at the Strand Theater.

The theater is air-conditioned and sufficiently large to allow each graduate to invite four guests. Tickets will be distributed to pupils on the morning of June 17. Since there are no reserved seats, I suggest that you try to arrive before 6:00 P.M. so that you can park easily and have your choice of seating.

Because of the large number of graduates, we ask your cooperation in the following details:

1. Do not send flowers to the school or theater. We do not have the staff or the room to handle them.

2. Do not come up to the stage to take pictures. I will be happy to remain after the ceremonies as long as necessary if you want to photograph your graduate officially receiving his or her diploma.

3. Please hold your applause until all the graduates receive their diplomas.

4. Remind your graduate to line up on the Maple Parkway side of the theater by 6:15 P.M.

5. Caps and gowns will be accepted in the gym office at any time on the day after graduation. Deposits will be returned at that time. The tassel may be kept as a souvenir.

This is a very happy occasion and I look forward to congratulating you in person at the ceremonies. Thank you again for your cooperation.

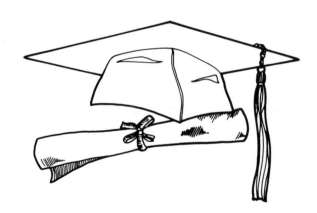

Letter 1–39: GUIDANCE

TO: Parents
FR: V. DiAngelo, Principal
RE: Guidance Services

Many parents have asked me for an explanation of the duties performed by our school guidance counselor. Some things an elementary guidance counselor does include:

1. Helping students to . . .
   understand their abilities and limitations
   adjust to a new school
   find answers to their concerns
   learn to make decisions
   develop skills in getting along with others

2. Talking with you about your child's . . .
   progress in school
   abilities and limitations
   growth and development

3. Helping teachers to . . .
   understand and meet individual student needs
   provide classroom guidance in such areas as self-understanding, decision making, and values
   find special help for students when needed
   plan units on guidance-related topics

4. Consulting with parents and teachers in private conferences about their children.

5. Coordinating referrals to school and community agencies when school personnel and parents agree this is needed.

6. Talking with children individually or in small groups. The child may request the counseling or may be referred by parents or teachers. Counseling is a voluntary service; no child is required to talk with the counselor.

Should you have any further questions, you may call the guidance office at 761-5924.

Letter 1–40: FIRST PAGE OF PARENT GUIDEBOOK

Dear Parents:

    I am happy to welcome you and your family to P.S. 54. Ours is a growing school that has been providing quality education to the Southwood community for over 20 years. Our experienced staff of teachers is dedicated to providing every child with the best educational opportunity possible. Many special services supplement our regular school program. These include:

_____

_____

_____

    We realize the importance of developing in each child an attitude of self-respect and self-worth. We try to provide a variety of opportunities for pupils to form meaningful and responsible relationships.

    Parents, we feel, are our partners in the important job of educating the children of this community. We welcome your suggestions and solicit your membership in the P.T.A. I can be reached at school by calling 761-5511.

_____

V. DiAngelo, Principal

Letter 1–41: HALLOWEEN

TO: Parents
FR: V. DiAngelo, Principal
RE: Halloween Safety

Halloween is a special day for children. It is a day they get to dress up in a variety of costumes and take to the streets, knocking on doors in search of special treats.

Traditionally, if a child does not receive a treat, he will play a trick. But in recent years, an increasing number of "tricks" have been played by adults on children, sometimes with tragic results.

Parents should take precautions against possible dangers their children may be exposed to. In the interest of encouraging wholesome fun along with safety, I am suggesting the following:

- A responsible adult should accompany all young children on their rounds, preferably before nightfall. If the rounds take place after dark, flashlights are recommended.

- Doorbell ringing should be limited to homes that are well lighted in anticipation of visits by little goblins and ghosts.

- Care should be taken to use sidewalks and avoid lawns where there may be objects to trip over.

- Stay away from the homes of known neighborhood cranks, who are the most likely to be planning some "tricks" of their own.

- Always cross streets at intersections after carefully looking both ways.

- Children should be forbidden to eat any gifts of food until they have returned home. All the treats should be carefully inspected, and fruit cut into small pieces, to make sure they do not harbor harmful objects. Candy that is broken, unwrapped, or wrapped loosely should be discarded. Popcorn in any form is a "no-no."

- Costumes should be made or bought with care. Make sure they are flame-retardant without loose folds to trip over. Reflective tape should be applied so an oncoming automobile will pick up the presence of a pint-sized witch, pirate, or clown.

- Masks can be hazardous because they limit a child's vision. A suggested substitute is colorful makeup based on a child's own design of how he or she wants to be disguised.

- Parents should use care in lighting jack-o'-lanterns with candles. They should be out of the reach of children.

By following these simple safety suggestions we can make sure that our children enjoy a colorful Halloween without any untoward event marring their fun.

Letter 1–42: PARENT AND STUDENT HANDBOOK

It is my pleasure to welcome you and your parents to P.S. 54. The teachers and staff join me in saying we are happy to have you as part of the P.S. 54 family. We hope this will be a successful and satisfying year for you.

The pages of this handbook are crammed with information that you will find useful about your school. Go through the entire handbook quickly at first. Then go back and read the pages that apply to you now. I suggest that parents and pupils read it together. Feel free to ask your teacher or guidance counselor for additional information on or explanation of the material in this handbook.

Be sure to acquaint yourself with the staff members listed on page three. These are out-of-classroom staff members who are here to help you get the most out of your years at P.S. 54. Parents will want to make note of the various phone numbers.

We are glad you are here!

Sincerely,

_____

V. DiAngelo, Principal

Letter 1–43: INTRODUCTION TO PARENT HANDBOOK

We are using this Handbook as a means of communicating between the home and school. There are many policies, regulations, and services discussed in these pages. Please read and keep this handbook readily available throughout the year.

Many of your questions have been anticipated and are discussed in some detail. We are always available to clarify any school matter. The telephone numbers listed for key staff members will prove helpful. Do not hesitate to use them.

Close cooperation between the home and school is essential to promote the best interests of the child. Parents are encouraged to visit school and to attend scheduled meetings of parents and teachers. Mutual benefits accrue when there is a meaningful exchange of information between home and school.

It is our hope that this Handbook will be helpful to you and that it will promote that understanding.

A parent or guardian is asked to detach and sign the receipt at the bottom of this sheet and return it to the child's teacher. Let us know what you think of this Handbook after the word "Comments."

Thank you,

_____
V.DiAngelo, Principal

Receipt

I have received the P.S. 54 Parent Handbook. My child is_____

in class _____.

_____
Signature

COMMENTS _____

_____

_____

_____

May 18, 19XX

To the parents of _____:

This is a special "thank you" in recognition of your child's contributions to our school newspaper. The many hours of after-school work and creative effort are appreciated by the faculty advisor, Ms. Larson-Davis, and by yours truly.

Sincerely,

_____

V. DiAngelo, Principal

Letter 1–45: HEAD LICE

November 17, 19XX
RE: Roxanne Cooperman
Class: 1C

Dear Mr. and Mrs. Cooperman:

Every year we find that a number of children return to school with a hair problem called pediculosis (nits). Every year we inspect the hair of every child in the school so as to avoid any serious spreading of the pediculosis condition.

When Mrs. Draekers, the school nurse, inspected Roxanne's hair, some nits were found. We are asking you to clear up the condition by using one of the shampoos prescribed by your physician, or available at your pharmacy. Note, too, that combing out the nits with a fine tooth comb is an important part of the treatment. It is the policy of this school to exclude all children who are found with nits (eggs) or lice. Make certain your child is free of both lice and nits before you send him/her back to school.

Sincerely,

_____
V. DiAngelo, Principal

---------------------------- Please detach and return to school ----------------------------

Dear Principal:

I have read the letter dated November 17 concerning head lice.

Child's Name: _____ Class: _____

_____
Parent's Signature

Letter 1–46: HEAD LICE

Dear Parents:

There has been some incidence of pediculosis (head lice) among the children in our school. We are examining the hair of suspected pupils and will be excluding from school for treatment those who are found to be affected.

It is each parent's responsibility to check the hair of their own children—daily.

It is expected that a temporary exclusion coupled with home treatment along the lines outlined below will be successful in ending any cases. Excluded pupils will be returned to school after treatment and inspection of the hair and scalp show elimination of the lice.

Your pharmacist can recommend a suitable product, or you may want to contact your physician. But shampoo is not enough—a fine-tooth comb must be used daily to remove the nits. Remember these three steps: Shampoo vigorously; rinse thoroughly; comb carefully.

Please understand that we have found only a few cases among our children. This is no reflection in any way upon a person's personal hygiene or cleanliness. This condition is found wherever large groups gather and can be picked up in any place upon contact with a person having such a condition. This letter is to make you aware rather than alarmed. Check your child daily.

Thank you for your cooperation.

Sincerely,

_____

V. DiAngelo, Principal

Some prevention hints:

1. Warn pupils not to lend their comb or brush to anyone. Have your child leave his or her comb and brush at home.

2. Keep hats, gloves, scarves, and so forth in book bags, instead of coat closets.

3. Check and launder child's coat, particularly those having pile or furlined collars or hoods.

4. Advise your child not to try on other children's hats or coats.

5. If you purchase or receive new clothing for your child, wash it before wearing.

6. You may want your child to bring a plastic shopping bag to school to keep his/her coat in.

Letter 1–47: HEAD LICE—SPANISH VERSION

TO: Parents of Pupils with Head Lice

   Examine la cabeza de cada miembro de la familia; en caso que se encuentre a alguien más con piojos o liendres, empiécese inmediatamente el tratamiento del cabello y cuero cabelludo, pues como bien saben, el piojo se pega.
   Cuando en la escuela se descubre que una niña or niño tiene piojos, liendres orgranos en la cabeza, inmediatamente se envia al hogar para que se someta al tratamiento que indicamos. Compre en la farmacía alguna preparación para matar piojos y liendres, pues hay muchos remedios eficaces.

_____

V. DiAngelo, Principal

Letter 1–48: HEALTH CHECK

TO: Parents
FR: V. DiAngelo, Principal
RE: Health Check

       To protect your child's health in school, he or she needs to have medical examinations at certain times during his or her school career, and to receive protective immunizations against disease. The requirements and recommendations of the Department of Health are listed below.

       Your family doctor is the best person to do the examinations. Please have your doctor complete the "Health History" and "Medical Report" below when he examines your child and give any necessary immunizations.

       If you prefer, you may have your child's medical examination and the necessary immunizations done at school. In this case, you yourself should complete the "Health History" below, and sign the form to request the services.

Health History

	Dates		Dates
Successful Smallpox Vaccination		Measles Vaccine	
Diphtheria-Tetanus or DPT		Rubella (German Measles)	
Polio: Salk Injections		Tuberculin Test	
Oral Monovalent		BCG Vaccination	
Oral Trivalent		Mumps	

Has the child had any of the following conditions? Check.

____Chicken Pox	____Frequent Colds	____Heart Trouble
____Measles	____Ear Infections	____Vision Defect
____Rubella	____Allergies	____Hearing Difficulty
____Mumps	____Convulsions	____TB
____Rheumatic Fever	____Orthopedic Defect	____Other

       If you do not have a family doctor, and wish these services to be given to your child in school, sign this form:

       I request that my child be given the health services for his present grade, described above.

_____	_____	_____
Signature of Parent	Address	Date

IMPORTANT: Smallpox vaccination must not be given while the child or anyone in the household has eczema or a skin rash. Does your child or anyone in your home have eczema or a rash? ____

Letter 1–49: HOME HABITS

TO: Parents
FR: V. DiAngelo, Principal
RE: Home Habits

There are many experiences that parents can provide at home that will help insure school success. Please review this checklsit. Look for opportunities to provide additional positive home habits.

1. Responsibility and Independence, and Caring for Self
   The parent/caregiver guides the child to:
   - put away toys and games
   - keep room neat
   - complete specific jobs/tasks
   - help set and clear the table
   - learn to button, zip, and tie shoelaces
   - learn to put on clothing, shoes, and socks
   - learn to select and hang up clothing
   - tend to bathroom and personal grooming needs

   Children should be praised for a job well done.

2. Getting Along with Others:
   The parent/caregiver:
   - makes arrangements for children to pay with others
   - teaches children how to share and respect other children's property
   - teaches children to accept other adults as friends
   - helps children learn to listen to others and follow directions

3. Routines
   The parent/caregiver:
   - designates appropriate times to go to bed, get up, eat, rest, and play that are consistent with children's needs and school schedules

4. Making Decisions
   Whenever opportunites arise, parents can allow children to plan activities or solve problems by encouraging decision-making. The choices should be kept simple: "Which book do you want me to read?" "Which game shall we play?" "Would you like an apple or a banana for a snack?"
   The way is left open for more than one suggestion so that the parent and child can discuss which might be best.

5. A Word on Television
   Television can be a learning experience if limited and used properly. There are many informative and educational programs, but too much television is not good for young children.
   When adults choose programs with children, an appropriate television viewing schedule can be planned. Choosing programs with care, and watching along with children help make television a more positive experience. Discussing favorite programs help children extend their vocabulary and concepts of the world around them.

Letter 1–50: HOMEWORK

Dear Parents:

Here are some thoughts on parent help at home and homework.

The purpose of homework is to extend and reinforce what has been learned in class and to develop a sense of self-discipline, personal responsibility and independent thinking.

We at P.S. 54 encourage parents to:

- show a positive interest in their children's homework as well as their school work.

- cooperate with the teacher to make homework more effective.

- provide children with a suitable place to do homework, away from TV or preschool children.

- serve as consultants about assignments, but not to do the assignments for the child.

- see that assignments are completed neatly.

- encourage but not pressure children.

- talk to their children about their attitudes toward school work and home-work.

In the interest of variety and in order to give pupils an opportunity to develop different kinds of skills, not all assignments will necessarily be written assignments. Some will be to read, to interview, to cut out, to collect, to study, to do research, to listen to a particular radio program or watch a special TV program.

Our school policy is, generally, not to give homework on weekends. Reason: to allow pupils to engage more fully in family activities.

Please feel free to consult your child's teacher whenever there is a question about homework. We want homework to be a help and not a punishment.

Yours truly,

_____

V. DiAngelo, Principal

Letter 1–51: HOMEWORK GUIDELINES

Dear Parents,

Homework serves an important purpose in your child's school life. It is a means of reviewing and reinforcing the lessons taught in school. Homework is also a way to help your child to develop work and study habits that will assist him or her throughout the years spent in school.

You can help your child develop some routines that will be of assistance in successfully completing homework assignments. The following suggestions are offered for this purpose.

1. Ask your child if he or she has homework that day. Be aware that homework is generally assigned every day except Friday or the day before a holiday. By asking your child about homework, you are helping him or her to remember that there is an assignment to be completed.

2. Become interested in your child's homework. Ask him or her to show the homework to you and to explain what the work completed was about. Sharing your child's work with him or her reinforces the importance of homework and helps the child to understand that you are interested in his or her progress. Looking at your child's homework also keeps you informed about the progress of the child and the way in which your child is able to complete the work assigned.

3. Remember that homework is your child's work—not yours. You should not do the work for the child; rather, you should be concerned with whether or not your child did the work. If your child has trouble with a homework assignment and cannot complete it, write a note telling the teacher about the problem. It is the teacher's responsibility to make the homework assignment clearly understood by each student.

4. Help your child set a regular homework time each day and remain with that commitment. Free your child of other responsibilities at that time.

5. Provide your child with a quiet place to work and study where he or she is not disturbed by younger children or pets.

Homework will help your youngster grow and develop.

Sincerely,

_____

V. DiAngelo, Principal

Letter 1–52: HOMEWORK GUIDELINES

Dear Parents,

The purpose of homework is to reinforce and extend what your child has learned in class and to develop a sense of self discipline, personal responsibility, and independent thinking. As a rule new material is not assigned for homework.

We hope the following information and suggestions will be helpful to you.

In order to give pupils an opportunity to develop various kinds of skills, teachers will give many types of homework assignments, some of which may not be written assignments. They may be to read, to cut out, to collect, to interview, to do research, to listen to a particular radio or TV program.

The school's policy is, generally, not to give homework on weekends. The reason for this is to give pupils a reward for a week's work well done and to allow them time to take part in family experiences such as trips, visits, outings, etc.

Time Allotments:
First grade–about 15 minutes a day
Second grade–about 20 minutes a day
Third grade–about 30 minutes a day
Fourth grade–about 40 minutes a day
Fifth grade–about 50 minutes a day

How You Can Help

1. Provide your child with a quiet place—at a table or desk—to work.
2. Set a regular time for doing homework each day and stick to it. Good times are just before or just after dinner. (Children should be given play time after school, before homework time.)
3. See that he brings home assignments clearly written down in his homework pad or in the back of his notebook.
4. Assist by offering helpful explanations and by seeing that homework is neat and complete. Never <u>do</u> an assignment for your child.
5. Offer encouragement; avoid pressure.
6. Have it understood that homework comes <u>before</u> TV.
7. Check with your child's teacher if an assignment is not clear.

Please feel free to consult the school whenever there is a question about homework, which, after all is intended to be a help, not a burden.

Yours truly,

_____

V. DiAngelo, Principal

Letter 1–53: HOMEWORK NOTICE

January 9, 19XX
RE: Billy deGroot
Class: 3B

Dear Mr. and Mrs. deGroot:

We consider homework to be an important part of your child's education. In spite of the efforts of Mr. Zimmerman, your child's teacher, Billy has not handed in several assignments. Some of the dates of missing homework include:

_____

_____

Homework is a factor in determining the grade received in the subject as well as providing lifelong skills. We urge your assistance in correcting this situation.

Sincerely,

_____

V. DiAngelo, Principal

--------------------------- Please detach and return to school ---------------------------

Pupil's Name: _____ Class: _____

I have read the homework notice dated: _____.

I would like to come in to talk about this on: _____.

Parent's comments: _____

_____

_____

_____

Parent's Signature

Letter 1–54: HONOR SOCIETY

March 15, 19XX

Dear Mr. and Mrs. Gleason:

Congratulations to you on Katherine's selection to the P.S. 54 Honor Society. Such a distinction is rightly shared by the parents who encouraged and nurtured the traits of character and perseverence that led to such an honor. I am confident that this is just one of many honors that Katherine will earn in the years ahead.

As you know, this award represents more than just scholastic achievement. Students are also evaluated for their school citizenship, service, and character.

It is a delight to have a student like Katherine in our school!

Sincerely,

_____

V. DiAngelo, Principal

Letter 1–55: IMPROVEMENT IN CLASS WORK

January 10, 19XX
RE: Carmella Maderi
Class: 1A

Dear Mr. and Mrs. Maderi:

I'm delighted to tell you that there has been a marked improvement in Carmella's class work. Her attitude toward school and increased effort has been noticed by her teacher, Mrs. Morris, and reported to me. This is good news and is due, in part, to your efforts and encourgement.

We have encouraged Carmella in school and hope that you will do the same at home. I did not hesitate to inform you when we saw a decline in effort and attitude in the past. It gives a great deal of pleasure to report this positive turn of events.

Of course, if this continues you will see better marks on the next report card. Thank you for your positive influence.

Sincerely,

_____

V. DiAngelo, Principal

Letter 1–56:   INCIDENT REPORT

April 3, 19XX
RE: Steve Schneider
Class: 7B

Dear Mr. and Mrs. Schneider:

Today, your son, ＿＿＿＿＿＿＿＿＿＿＿ was involved in the following

incident in school: ＿＿＿＿＿＿＿＿＿＿＿＿＿＿＿＿＿＿＿＿＿＿＿＿＿＿＿＿＿

＿＿＿＿＿＿＿＿＿＿＿＿＿＿＿＿＿＿＿＿＿＿＿＿＿＿＿＿＿＿＿＿＿＿＿＿＿＿＿

＿＿＿＿＿＿＿＿＿＿＿＿＿＿＿＿＿＿＿＿＿＿＿＿＿＿＿＿＿＿＿＿＿＿＿＿＿＿＿

＿＿＿＿＿＿＿＿＿＿＿＿＿＿＿＿＿＿＿＿＿＿＿＿＿＿＿＿＿＿＿＿＿＿＿＿＿＿＿

This took place at ＿＿＿＿＿＿ o'clock, during ＿＿＿＿＿＿＿＿＿＿. The
staff member supervising the children at that time was Mr. Marchetti.

＿＿＿ We tried to reach you by telephone but were unsuccessful because:

＿＿＿＿＿＿＿＿＿＿＿＿＿＿＿＿＿＿＿＿＿＿＿＿＿＿＿＿＿＿＿＿＿＿＿＿＿＿＿

＿＿＿ We gave your child the following first aid: ＿＿＿＿＿＿＿＿＿＿＿

＿＿＿＿＿＿＿＿＿＿＿＿＿＿＿＿＿＿＿＿＿＿＿＿＿＿＿＿＿＿＿＿＿＿＿＿＿＿＿

If you want any more information about this incident, please call the school at
761-7644 and ask to speak to Mr. Marchetti.
We would appreciate your keeping the school up to date as far as:

＿＿＿ current phone number

＿＿＿ current work number

＿＿＿ name of relative or neighbor we can call in case of an emergency

Thank you.

Sincerely,

＿＿＿＿＿＿＿＿＿＿＿＿＿＿＿＿＿＿＿

V. DiAngelo, Principal

Letter 1-57: SPECIFIC INCIDENT

Dear Parents of P.S. 54 Students:

We rarely write letters to be sent to all parents. However, on occasion, it is necessary that all parents receive some word of school action.

As you know we have had disturbances in P.S. 54 in the last few days. We have investigated these thoroughly and we can say absolutely that the incidents are not racial in nature although both whites and blacks have been involved. The problem is one between residents of different areas of the community. Significantly, both blacks and whites from the Millburn area have been fighting with whites and blacks from the Clarkston area. The situation, then, is one of area, not race.

We have taken a number of steps to deal with present disturbances and to prevent future outbreaks.

(1) We have identified and suspended from school all those who have taken a leadership role in the disturbances. These students will remain out of school until we are assured that calm has been restored. None of these students will be readmitted until the student and his parents have had a personal meeting with the building principal, Mr. DiAngelo.

(2) Each student now suspended for his role in the disturbances will be notified that any further activity of this nature, will result in an expulsion hearing before the Board of Education with all that this implies.

(3) We have assigned a number of additional teachers to the P.S. 54 building. These teachers are drawn from other duties, such as guidance, in other schools. This does pose a hardship in those buildings, but we think they are more needed right now in P.S. 54. These teachers will be assigned to hall supervision and other duties designed to be certain that there are no more disturbances. They will be withdrawn from P.S. 54 when it seems reasonable to do so.

(4) Our Student Intergroup Education Committee is now meeting with representative students from both troubled areas, and with other students, to try to define the problems that exist. More important, this Committee will make recommendations for change based on their findings and they have been assured, by me, that these recommendations will be fully considered.

(5) We have not called in the police in this matter and we will not call in the police in future incidents if it is at all possible to avoid doing so. We believe these problems should be handled by the school personnel when possible.

There will be a meeting at P.S. 54 at 8 P.M. on January 13, 19XX. Please attend. We need your help and your support.

Sincerely,

_____

V. DiAngelo, Principal

Letter 1-58: KINDERGARTEN WELCOME

Dear Parents:

We are happy to admit your child to our Kindergarten. We know that the experiences and learnings he will receive will give him a good start on his school career.

During the summer try to acquaint your child with the idea of being away from you for progressively longer periods of time.

ORIENTATION

In order to introduce your child to school, we hold half sessions for the first two days. In September, for the first two days, half the children attend during the A.M. session and half will attend during the P.M. session.

REGULAR SESSIONS

Regular Kindergarten sessions will begin in September. (Date will be announced before the end of the school year.) After the first two days of orientation, all children will report for the full session.

Several days prior to the opening of school, post cards will be sent indicating your child's Kindergarten class and teacher. The time for the shortened session for orientation for your child will also be stated. Your child must bring this card with him when he reports to school. Children who do not appear by Wednesday, after the first day of school, will not be placed unless the school has been apprised of the child's inability to attend.

We have found that children make a much better school adjustment if parents do not escort them into the building or yard on the first days of school. Therefore, you will leave your child at the Davis Avenue courtyard gates with the monitors if the weather is clear. In case of rain, you will escort your child as far as the Davis Avenue door where monitors will meet them.

Yours very truly,

_____

V. DiAngelo, Principal

Letter 1–59: KINDERGARTEN PARENT QUESTIONNAIRE

Child's Name _____
                               Last   First

Address _____

_____

Telephone Number _____

Has your child had any previous school experience? _____

If so, when? _____ For how long? _____

Where? _____

Can your child dress him or herself? ____ Tie shoes? ____

Does your child have any special interests or hobbies? _____

What are they? _____

_____

Does your child have any special talent(s)? _____

What are they? _____

_____

What kinds of activities does your child seem to enjoy most? _____

_____

_____

What are your child's feelings about coming to school? _____

_____

_____

What are your questions and concerns? _____

_____

_____

COMMENTS: _____

_____

_____

Letter 1–60: KINDERGARTEN CURRICULUM

TO: Parents of Kindergarten Children

Now that you have registered your child for next September's Kindergarten at P.S. 54, you probably would like to know what to expect.

In Kindergarten your child will learn:

- to recognize full name, telephone number, address, birthday, and age.
- to recognize colors
- to do handwork (cutting, pasting, coloring, painting)
- to express ideas through dramatic play and other creative activities
- to understand calendar concepts—i.e., days of the week
- to recognize numerals and small groups of objects by counting, and to count by rote
- to understand the meaning of one, two, three, four, five and of first, second, etc.
- to match circles, squares, triangles and other shapes
- to draw a given number of objects
- to tell a story suggested by a picture
- to retell a story, following a sequence of events
- to repeat fingerplays, nursery rhymes, and poems
- to enjoy books through looking at books and listening to stories
- to follow left-to-right progression required for reading
- to differentiate between likenesses and differences in pictures, letters, and words
- to recognize alphabet letters and words that begin with the same sound
- to recognize and print name and show interest in labels and signs
- to develop awareness of plants, animals, seasons, and the world around him/her
- to begin to read and handle numbers with comfort

Letter 1-61: SCHEDULE FOR KINDERGARTEN

TO: Parents of Kindergarten Pupils

MY KINDERGARTEN SCHEDULE

I will be in the _____ class.

My first day will be _____

                 Time: _____
I will spend my first day getting acquainted with my teacher and school.
I should come to school just before the bell rings.
I will learn to be on time.
I will go directly home when I am dismissed.

I will ride Bus # _____. My driver's name is _____.

My teacher's name is _____
Lunch money will be collected on Wednesdays.

The price of milk is _____ per week.

The price of lunch is _____ per week.

Letter 1–62: CLOTHING FOR KINDERGARTEN

August 21, 19XX

Dear Parents,

Parents often ask about the kind of school clothes a child should wear. They realize that the Kindergarten child particularly needs to feel comfortable and free in work and play activities. Here are some helpful hints:

- Choose simple washable play clothes for inside school, warm and serviceable clothes for outside.
- Buy clothes that your child can manage—big enough to get on easily, big buttons and buttonholes, big loops for hanging coats and sweaters, large rubbers, boots and overshoes, mittens fastened to coat or jacket, and simple, easy-to-manage underwear.

Label everything removable (snowsuit, rubbers, mittens, boots, coats, caps, sweaters). You may use name tapes or adhesive tape lettered with indelible ink. A special color, mark or sticker inside boots or rubbers will tell your child which one goes on which foot. Find a way to attach mittens firmly to the jacket or coat. Mitten clips are fine.

Kindergarteners are taught to take care of clothes and materials, but paint does spill and clay and paste do smear. When dressed for work, children don't worry. Your child's teacher may suggest that you send certain materials for use in class.

Yours truly,

_____

V. DiAngelo, Principal

Letter 1–63: KINDERGARTEN GRADUATION

June 1, 19XX

Dear Parents of Kindergarten Pupils:

The year has passed so quickly. The little people who came into school in September for the first time are now sophisticated school pupils with many happy memories of the All Day Kindergarten.

We would like to invite you to a special program on Tuesday, June 19, 19XX. We call this our Kindergarten "Graduation" and every pupil will receive a diploma.

Because we have seven classes, the graduates are arranged in two groups. Ceremonies will take place in the school auditorium. At the end of the program parents are encouraged to take the "graduate" out for a treat. School will resume for them on Wednesday, and continue through June 27.

Group I children and guests will come to school at 8:40 A.M. Children will go directly to the classroom, and guests will get seats in the Auditorium.

Group II children and guests are to go to their classroom at 10:15 A.M. where monitors will greet you. As soon as the 9 A.M. ceremony is over the teachers will join the pupils in the classroom and the parents and guests will be seated in the Auditorium.

Congratulations on reaching this milestone!

Sincerely,

_____

V. DiAngelo, Principal

Group I –K1-207)
       K3-211)
       K5-213)   will perform at 9:00 A.M.
       K7-113)
Group II–K2-203)
       K4-205)   will perform at 10:30 A.M.
       K6-212)

Letter 1–64: LATENESS

December 1, 19XX
RE: Carol Raznozian
Class: 6A

Dear Mr. and Mrs. Raznozian:

A check of your child's record shows that she has been late on eight occasions this school year. Repeated lateness is harmful both to your child's education and to the class that is disturbed.

Most recent latenesses include these dates: _____

_____

_____

I am very anxious to meet with you to discuss this problem and hopefully arrive at a satisfactory solution. Please call me for an appointment at 761-5511.

Sincerely,

_____

V. DiAngelo, Principal

Letter 1–65: PARENT LIBRARY REPORT

TO: Parents
RE: Parent Library Report

Many of our parents have made books a part of shared parent-child experiences. In order to encourage increased reading on the part of pupils during their leisure time we have come up with this Parent Library Report. For Early Childhood classes we call this "List of Books and Stories Read Aloud to My Child." For older pupils it can be titled, "List of Books Read by My Child at Home."

List of Books and Stories Read Aloud to My Child.

Child's Name: _____ Class: _____ Date: _____

During the month of _____ I read the following books and stories to my child. I have placed a check alongside those titles that he/she enjoyed the most.

Author   Title

_____   _____

_____   _____

_____   _____

_____   _____

_____   _____

_____   _____

_____   _____

_____   _____

                                            _____
                                            Parent's Signature

Letter 1–66: LIBRARY BOOKS

March 5, 19XX

Dear Mr. and Mrs. Gomez:

Please have your son, Michael, return Make Way for Ducklings tomorrow. It was borrowed from our library on February 5.

When this book comes back, your child will be able to take another fine book home.

The other children would like to have a chance to take home Make Way for Ducklings, also.

Thank you for your cooperation.

Sincerely,

V. DiAngelo, Principal

Letter 1–67: LIBRARY BOOKS—SPANISH VERSION

_____, 19XX

Estimado (a) _____:

    Tenga la bondad de devolver el libro _____

mañana. El libro fué cogido de nuestra biblioteca el _____.
    Cuando el libro sea devuelto su nino podrá coger otro prestado para llevarlo
casa.
    Los otros ninos también tienen el deseo de llevar a su casa el libro_____.
Muchas gracias por su cooperación.

               Atentamente,

               _____

               V. DiAngelo, Principal

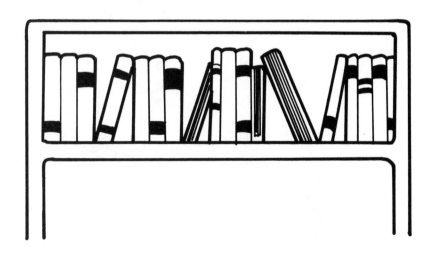

Letter 1–68: SCHOOL LUNCH RULES

Dear Parents:

Because of the large numbers of pupils eating in school and our limited space and personnel, we must enforce certain rules strictly. While some of these rules seem basic, there are many children who forget them when they eat lunch in school.

In order to help reinforce the manners they are taught at home, Mrs. Washington will be keeping some children in after school. You will be notified if your child is being kept in.

Please review these rules with your child if he or she eats in school.

V. DiAngelo, Principal

1. Pupils who eat in school may not leave the yard during the lunch hour.
2. Pupils must be respectful to all school personnel, teachers, aides, and lunchroom workers.
3. Pupils may not take food from another pupil's tray.
4. Pupils must stay in their assigned grade area in the yard. Fifth graders will stay in their class areas.
5. Pupils must not throw food or blow paper through straws.
6. Talking must be conversational; no shouting.
7. No running, kicking, or fighting.
8. Tables are for food trays. No crawling under tables or walking on benches or tables.
9. When in the school yard pupils may not climb fences, walls, or basketball hoops.
10. Pupils in grades one through four are not to use any balls or other equipment.
11. Violators of school rules will not be able to eat in school.
12. The best discipline is self-discipline.

Letter 1–69: LUNCHROOM BEHAVIOR

February 22, 19XX

TO: Parent of Cecelia Griffen   Class: 4B
RE: Lunch Behavior

Your daughter Cecelia has not been behaving properly during the lunch period. This has been brought to my attention by Mrs. Washington. Some of the things taking place include the following:

_____

_____

If there is no improvement we shall be obliged to ask you to come to school to sit with your child during lunch. We have already told your daughter of the violations involved. Please discuss these items with your child. Working together I am sure we can bring about an improvement.

Sincerely,

_____

V. DiAngelo, Principal

----------------------- DETACH AND RETURN TO SCHOOL -----------------------

Dear Principal:

I have read your note concerning my son's/daughter's behavior during the lunch period.

_____   _____

Date   Parent's Signature

Letter 1–70: LUNCH NOTICE

October 12, 19XX

Dear Mr. and Mrs. Wisnofski:

Your child Bill of Class 7A was reported for:

_____ throwing food

_____ running

_____ shouting

_____ pushing

_____ fighting

_____ disobeying adults

_____ other:

I'm sure you agree that such behavior endangers his safety, and the safety of other children. We feed approximately 200 pupils at that time. It is imperative that we have the cooperation of all the pupils in the lunchroom. Please speak to Bill about this matter.

Sincerely,

_____

V. DiAngelo, Principal

--------------------------- Please return to you child's teacher ---------------------------

I have received your notice dated _____ about _____'s behavior in

the lunchroom.

Comments: _____

_____

_____   _____   _____

Parent's Signature   Child's Name   Class

Letter 1-71: LUNCH EXCLUSION

September 30, 19XX

Dear Mr. and Mrs. Kim:

Your daughter, Li, of Class 4B has been barred from eating in the lunchroom for a week beginning October 9 because her behavior is endangering the health and

safety of the other children. In spite of warnings, she ＿＿＿＿＿＿＿＿＿＿＿

＿＿＿＿＿＿＿＿＿＿＿＿＿＿＿＿＿＿＿＿＿＿＿＿＿＿＿

＿＿＿＿＿＿＿＿＿＿＿＿＿＿＿＿＿＿＿＿＿＿＿＿＿＿＿

Please make arrangements for your child to eat elsewhere or she will be placed in a special room for the entire lunch period. Since she will not be permitted to enter the lunchroom, it will be necessary for you to provide a cold lunch for her.

Please detach and return the bottom part of this letter. Also, include your phone number since we were not able to reach you on the telephone.

Yours truly,

＿＿＿＿＿＿＿＿＿＿＿＿＿＿

V. DiAngelo, Principal

----------------------- DETACH AND RETURN TO SCHOOL ----------------------

Dear Principal:

I have read your letter regarding my son's/daughter's lunchroom behavior. I understand he/she must not eat in the lunchroom during the week of

＿＿＿＿＿＿＿＿＿＿.

＿＿＿＿＿＿＿＿＿＿＿＿＿＿

Parent's Signature

Letter 1-72: LUNCH MONEY

TO: Selected Parents
RE: Request for Lunch Money

Some pupils forget to bring their lunch to school. Frequently they have no money with them with which to purchase the school lunch. When that happens we serve the pupil a lunch of peanut butter and jelly sandwich along with a container of milk. We ask that the pupil bring the modest cost of 50¢ to the lunchroom aide the next morning.

Your child, _____, in Class _____, did

not have any lunch or lunch money on _____. Please send in the fifty cents with your child tomorrow. Thank you.

Sincerely,

_____

V. DiAngelo, Principal

Letter 1–73: CHILDREN'S MAGAZINES

TO: Parents
FR: V. DiAngelo, Principal
RE: Children's Magazines

     Today there are many contemporary children's magazines that will stretch your child's imagination and make reading fun. Not every magazine is appropriate for every child. Before you actually subscribe to any magazine, make sure that it appeals to your son or daughter. You will also want to find out whether special introductory subscription rates are available for new subscribers.

     Here is a letter you might want to use in making your request:

---

                            street address
                            city, state, zip
                            date

magazine
address
city, state, zip

Dear Editor:

     _____ Magazine has been brought to my attention. I am planning to enter a subscription for my son/daughter. I would like to have a copy of your magazine to show to my child. I would greatly appreciate your sending me a sample copy along with current subscription rates. Thank you.

                            Yours truly,

Letter 1–74: MATHEMATICS—
HOW YOU, THE PARENT, CAN HELP

Dear Parents:

There are many ways you can help your child at home in order to make him more math conscious.

Here are a few suggestions:

In the Kitchen

1. Following recipes—make half as much, twice as much, etc.
2. Measuring out liquids—"How many glasses of milk can we get from this container?"
3. Measuring numbers of pieces—"How many sandwiches can we make from this loaf of bread?"
4. Estimating number of beans in a package, crackers in a box, etc.

Shopping

1. Estimating amount of money needed to buy meat for the week, groceries for the week, etc.
2. Comparing sizes and weights of packages.
3. Comparing prices of large amounts versus smaller amounts.
4. Estimating weights of oranges, apples, etc.
5. Figuring price of one item if they are 2 for _____, or 3 for _____.
6. Estimating the sum of the bill at the register.

Travelling

1. Estimating distance travelled.
2. Computing mileage covered.
3. Keeping a record of things observed along the way—e.g. number of blue cars, VW's, etc. passed in five minutes.
4. Identifying varying geometric shapes (stop signs, yield signs, etc.)
5. Computing mileage per gallon car delivers.
6. Comparing gasoline prices, taxes.
7. Figuring distances on road maps.

$$\begin{array}{r} 2 \\ +\ 2 \\ \hline 4 \end{array}$$

Temperature

Comparing temperatures:
        indoors with outdoors
        winter with summer
        one day with the next
Computing average temperatures—weekly, monthly.

Clothing

        Noting and comparing sizes and measurements.
        Comparing prices.
        Computing cost of a daily wardrobe.

Family Finance

        Helping to plan the family budget.
        Discussing problems or decisions to be made, including alternatives.
        Helping to balance checking account.
        Figuring cost of family entertainment.

Keep In Mind

        Always try to find a reasonable estimate before trying to compute the answer to any problem.
        Computation is a rote skill; estimation is a thinking guess.

        Yours truly,

        _____

        V. DiAngelo, Principal

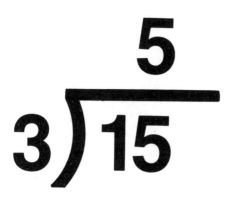

Letter 1–75: NEW MATH PROGRAM

Dear Parent:

Many times parents ask us about the "new" math. It scares them and keeps them from helping their children at home. While the textbooks and other learning materials we use do contain new approaches, the fact remains that 2 plus 2 still equals 4. Here are some suggestions for helping your child at home feel more comfortable and successful with numbers:

1. Let your child help you to:
    a. double check your register tape from the supermarket.
    b. find your train on the timetable.
    c. help measure for a do-it-yourself project.
    d. figure cooking recipes.
    e. keep track of oil, gas, mileage on trips.
    f. plan the route on a road map.
    g. check the temperature.
    h. read the barometer.
    i. help make out bank deposit slips.
    j. check your cancelled checks with you.
    k. go over floor plans of new house or carpeting purchase.

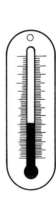

2. Give him or her numbers in play times, such as:
    a. puzzle books and dominoes
    b. quick mental drills with number facts.
    c. card games involving numbers
    d. word puzzles involving number concepts.

3. Don't pass on your dislike for mathematics to your child; you will solve nothing by telling him or her that you "hated fractions," or "math is for boys."

4. Help him or her see ways in which math is used in the modern world:
    a. making tall buildings stand up
    b. rockets, jets, and space flights
    c. banking and insurance careers
    d. computer technology

5. Help him or her solve simple problems. Help your child learn to estimate or approximate answers. This will avoid ridiculous responses.

Sincerely,

_____

V. DiAngelo, Principal

Letter 1–76: MEDICATION IN SCHOOL

Dear Parents:

Students needing occasional medications, such as penicillin, etc., for colds, earaches and sore throats, are to take those medications at home if possible. Medication that is prescribed three (3) times a day can be given before the student comes to school, after school, and again at bedtime.

Medications to be given at school must have a completed medication instruction form. Forms for your doctor to fill out may be obtained from the principal. ALL medication that comes into the school must be turned in to the principal or school nurse.

Any medication sent to school without proper identification will NOT be given.

We ask your cooperation as we are primarily concerned with the safety and health of your child. Our school nurse, Mrs. Draekers, can be seen in Room 103.

Thank you.

V. DiAngelo, Principal

Letter 1–77: MEDICATION REQUEST FORM

This form is designed to assure parents and protect children in need of receiving medication during the school day or school activity appropriate handling of such needs. The general contents of the form have been reviewed by the Department of Public Instruction of the Department of Health. The School District does not in any way want to discourage parents from dispensing or supervising medication to their children at school if they are able to do so, but is assisting only as an alternative.

Date: _____

Student's Name: _____ School: _____

I hereby give my permission to the staff at _____

school to dispense medication prescribed by Dr. _____

for my child, beginning _____ ; ending _____
                        Date   Date

Name of medication or prescription number (including drug store):

_____

Special instructions for dispensing: _____

_____

If there are any side effects of this medication, please indicate:

_____

_____   _____
Physician's Signature   Parent or Guardian

Letter 1–78: NEW PROGRAM

Dear Parents,

Education is an ongoing process. Methods and techniques are constantly undergoing revision in order to insure the best possible education for your child. In today's society where there is so much to learn, it is essential that your children be taught in the most efficient and effective manner possible.

Toward that goal, a new program of reading instruction is under consideration for use in our elementary school. It is a program that has been used with great success in many localities, and one which we hope will prove beneficial in our district.

Since the ability to read is so fundamental to success in all areas of education as well as life itself, this is not a step we have taken without a great deal of testing and evaluation. We sincerely believe that this program will be the best for your child and all the children of our district.

Since the program is far too long to explain in a letter, we will be holding a meeting of all concerned parents on Wednesday, October 1 at 8:00 P.M. in the school auditorium. At that time, the entire program will be explained and discussed, and any questions you may have will be answered.

You are cordially invited to attend. We look forward to meeting you at that time and have the opportunity for explaining this program to you.

I hope to see you there.

Sincerely,

_____

V. DiAngelo, Principal

Letter 1-79: FINAL MESSAGE FOR PARENT NEWSLETTER

Congratulations to our graduates! It is our hope that their experience at P.S. 54 has brought us together in a meaningful way so that graduates, their parents, and our faculty have been best served. It is our sincere wish that our warm and fruitful relationship be maintained.

May I take this opportunity to welcome the children who are entering our school in the fall. Parents can be helpful in making the adjustment of our younger pupils to school life smooth and rewarding. You are urged to cooperate with the school in following a few simple routines and requirements.

Every child currently attending kindergarten and first grade will receive a slip of paper at the end of the year. This paper will have the child's name, new class, new room number, and the first date to report to school—September 8. All kindergarten and first grade classes can be easily located on the first floor. Upper grade pupils will have this information on their report cards.

On the first day of school, parents should bring the children directly to their rooms. The room numbers are posted over the doors. If you have any difficulty, any member of the staff will help you. After a few days, all kindergarten and first grade classes will line up in their appointed places on the first floor. It is best that you arrive with your child at about 8:30 A.M.

It has been a pleasure for me to work with the children and parents of P.S. 54 during the past year. I trust you will enjoy a most refreshing and healthy summer and return on September 8 for another gratifying school year.

Sincerely,

_____

V. DiAngelo, Principal

Letter 1–80: RETENTION

January 22, 19XX
RE: Marcia Kramer
Class: 5A

Dear Mr. and Mrs. Kramer:

Each year at this time we take a close look at the records of those pupils who may not be promoted at the end of the school year. A check of your child's marks indicates that she is not meeting our standards for promotion in June.

When talking to her teacher(s) the following items were mentioned as possible reasons for failure:

_____ poor test results   _____ not working up to ability

_____ lack of class participation   _____ wasted class time

_____ resentful of help   _____ disturbing behavior

_____ missing homework   _____ late to class

_____ poor attendance

Because of your positive attitude in the past we are appealing to you now to take the necessary steps to insure your child's promotion. This notice is being sent to you now so that enough time remains for your child to improve in time to be promoted to the next grade.

By calling 761-7644, you can make an appointment to meet with me or your child's guidance counselor, Mrs. Perez.

Thank you for giving this matter your immediate attention.

Sincerely,

_____

V. DiAngelo, Principal

Letter 1–81: PARENTS' OBSERVATION FORM

Dear Parents:

We are attempting to provide each child with an individual program that will offer instruction based upon individual student needs. The statements below represent important ingredients of a good program.

<u>Directions</u>: Please check the most appropriate line based upon your observation. Mark only the ones that you are able to observe.

Usually	Quite often	Occasionally	Almost never	
——	——	——	——	1. Children work with a variety of materials.
——	——	——	——	2. The teacher works with individual children.
——	——	——	——	3. Not everyone is doing the same thing.
——	——	——	——	4. Children are being tested throughout the building.
——	——	——	——	5. Students move about the classrooms working on their own assignments.
——	——	——	——	6. Individual student progress records are used.
——	——	——	——	7. Classrooms seem to be well organized and students work with a minimum of direction.

Letter 1–82: OPEN SCHOOL WEEK

Dear Parents,

There is much to be gained when parents and teachers meet, face to face, to discuss the progress of pupils. You will have several opportunities to do this during the current school year, in addition to the afternoon Fall Conference on November 13 and the afternoon Spring Conference on April 13.

We hope that all parents will take advantage of this opportunity. As in the past, one evening conference is planned for Tuesday evening, November 18. It is suggested that only those parents who cannot come in the afternoon attend the evening conference. Parents of kindergarten and first grade children will have a chance to confer with their children's teachers on Thursday, November 12. When you attend these sessions we hope that you will speak frankly to the teacher and listen attentively to the teacher's report on how your child acts in school. You should be interested in learning how another caring adult perceives your child.

American Education Week, commonly referred to as Open School Week, will be observed from November 17 through November 21. At this time, you are invited to see your child's class in action. For many of you it will be a real eye-opener to observe the group dynamics that take place in a classroom. You will see how age peers of your child interact with one another and their teacher. Please do not bring preschool age children with you. We want very much to avoid disturbing the usual classroom routines and deportment.

Please make full use of these opportunities to learn more about your child and his or her school life.

Sincerely,

_____

V. DiAngelo, Principal

Letter 1–83: OPEN SCHOOL WEEK

November 6, 19XX

Dear Parents:

      You are cordially invited to visit your child's class during Open School Week, November 17 through November 21. The theme for this year is "Our Future Is in Our Schools." You are welcome whenever you can come during this week. No pass is required at this time.

      Since this visit is designed to let you see your child and his/her classmates at work, the teacher has been requested not to engage in conversation with any parent during this visit. Please cooperate by entering the classroom quietly and by taking a place at the back of the room. Do not distract the class and teacher by walking around to inspect displays or to talk to a child.

      The opportunity to inspect your child's work, to meet the teacher, and to discuss your child's progress will be given on two other dates this month. A special notice will be sent to you regarding these dates.

      I sincerely hope that you will avail yourselves of the opportunity to visit and acquaint yourself with your child's work in school.

Sincerely yours,

_____

V. DiAngelo, Principal

-------------------- Please tear off and return to your child's teacher --------------------

I have received the notice dated November 6th regarding Open School Week and have made note of the contents.

_____   _____ _____

Child's Name   Class   Parent's Signature

Letter 1–84: ORIENTATION

TO: Parents of New Pupils   September, 19XX

Child's Name _____   Classroom _____

  Greetings from Public School 54. We expect to open on schedule on Monday, September 8. We will open with about 700 children including classes from Kindergarten through Grade 8.

  We hope that the following information will be helpful to you and your child in getting started at P.S. 54.

Arrival Procedures

  Children will line up in the school yard and go up to their classrooms when the bell rings at 8:35 A.M. When the weather is cold or inclement, the children will assemble in the cafeteria. A pupil who arrives after 8:45 A.M. is marked late.

Procedure on Dismissal

  Parents will be notified in advance if there is to be an early dismissal. Kindergarten children will be dismissed at exit 6. Grades 1 through 5 will be dismissed at exits 3 and 4. Special Education Classes will be dismissed from the exits nearest their classrooms.

Notices

  The school and the P.T.A. communicate with parents by sending notices home with the children. Ask your child regularly if he/she has such a notice. Some notices or forms will need to be filled out or may require a signature. Please try to have these returned the following day.

Illness

  If your child should become ill in school, you will be contacted to come and take him/her home. It is important that you notify the school when you have a change of address or telephone number (at home or business) and if there is a change in the name or telephone number of the person to be contacted if you are not available.

  Keep your child home if he/she is not feeling well or has a temperature.

Parent Visits to School

  Parents are urged to attend meetings which will be held to inform them about the school's instructional programs and which will enable them to learn how they can help the school educate their children. Individual conferences between a parent, a teacher or a supervisor can be arranged by calling or writing for an appointment. The school telephone number is 761-7644.

  All visitors to the school, including parents, must use the main entrance on Davis Avenue and go directly to Room 103 before proceeding to their destination.

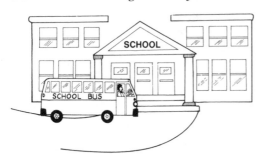

_____

V. DiAngelo, Principal

Letter 1–85: PERMISSION FOR PSYCHOLOGICAL SERVICES

January 11, 19XX
RE: Lee Montoya
Class: 8B

Dear Mr. and Mrs. Montoya:

I am writing to confirm our discussion of January 8, 19XX. At that time we outlined to you all of the compelling reasons that convince us that your son, Lee, should be seen by a member of our child study team.

At that time we pointed out that general school performance, classroom behavior, and the initial interview by the school psychologist indicated that Lee would benefit from counseling by our school psychologist. This was confirmed by the comments made by Dr. Gligor.

Fortunately, our school receives the services of a school psychologist on Tuesday and Thursday each week. Your son, Lee, will be seen by Dr. Gligor. You are welcome to come in to meet Dr. Gligor at any mutually convenient time. He will also be happy to discuss relevant matters with you on the telephone or by note whenever you wish. This is a valuable service that I am glad you wish to take advantage of.

Please sign the enclosed permission form and return it to school as soon as possible. All matters concerning this counseling will be kept strictly confidential. If I can be of further help, please call.

Sincerely,

_____

V. DiAngelo, Principal

Letter 1–86: PERMISSION TO BE PHOTOGRAPHED

October 7, 19XX

Dear Parents of Grade 6 Students:

On October 18, 19XX we expect a photographer from <u>The Southwood Journal</u> to be at our school to photograph pupils participating in the following event:

_____ school play

_____ sports event

_____ award ceremony

_____ pupil interview

_____ other: _____

Your child's photograph may or may not appear in the newspaper. Before allowing your child to be photographed we would like to have your permission. I'm sure your child will be happy to see his/her photo in print. The decision to include the photo is, of course, made by the <u>Journal</u>.

Sincerely,

_____

V. DiAngelo, Principal

------------------------------------ Detach and Return ------------------------------------

Dear Principal:

I give my permission to have my child _____ photographed as described in your letter dated October 7, 19XX.

_____

Parent's Signature

Letter 1–87: STUDENT PROGRESS

Dear Parents:

How is your child progressing in reading?

Besides your informal observation there are five criteria you can apply. Ask yourself these questions. We have included some positive responses to each question.

Test Scores

Have your child's scores on vocabulary and reading tests significantly improved?

Scores on these tests should go up considerably even in a short period of time. For example, after working on the program for one year, your child might advance two or three years in reading ability. Scores like these would show that your child's ability increased two or three times faster than would be expected.

There is a way you can find out exactly how fast your child is becoming a better reader. Your child's guidance counselor at school will be able to help you get this information.

Ask the guidance counselor to give your child a reading test (with vocabulary and reading comprehension sections) before you start your program. Arrange for your child to be re-tested in about six months with a different "form" (or version) of the first test.

You will get the most clear and accurate picture of your child's reading progress by comparing these "before" and "after" scores. A substantial improvement (twelve to eighteen months in six months' time) is proof that your program is having a tremendous effect.

Reading Habits

Have your child's reading habits changed as a result of the program?

The program directs your child to find new words while reading. However, the real measure of success is whether your child develops an interest in reading for his own enjoyment. He should not read just to satisfy you!

Work and Study Habits

Have your child's work and study habits improved?

The program encourages him to work in an organized, efficient way. He should begin to do his assignments from school in the same conscientious manner.

Report Card Marks

Have your child's marks gone up?

As your child becomes a better reader, his marks should also improve. High marks in English, social studies, and science indicate that a child reads well.

Self-Image

Has there been a change in your child's feelings about himself?

As his reading ability and schoolwork improve, he should think more highly of himself, and appear to be a happier, more confident child.

The program described in this handbook can make your life more pleasurable and rewarding too! You will be thrilled to watch your child improve and become a better reader under your direction. You will have the satisfaction of knowing that your help made all the difference.

Letter 1–88: PROMOTION ON TRIAL

September 23, 19XX
RE: Gary Swartz
Class: 3B

Dear Mr. and Mrs. Swartz:

As we discussed in June, Gary was promoted on trial from Grade 2 to Grade 3. We are convinced that this move is in his best interests if he works to succeed. We want to be sure that you know the conditions of his promotion.

If, by the end of the first marking period, Gary's teachers feel that he cannot succeed in his school work, or if he appears to be too immature for his surroundings, it may be necessary to transfer him back to Grade 2.

We would only make a decision of this sort after consultation with you, his guidance counselor, and his teachers. This would only be done if we were convinced it was in Gary's best interests.

Right now we are optimistic that with cooperation between home and school, your son will do fine in the higher grade. Please call me at 761-5511 if you have any questions.

Sincerely,

_____

V. DiAngelo, Principal

Letter 1–89:   READING

TO: Parents
RE: Reading—How the Parent Can Help

Teaching reading is an important and difficult job in which both the school and the parent can cooperate.

Here are many ways in which you can help your child.

1. <u>Talk</u> to your child.

   Almost from the day he is born, a child is ready to express himself. At first he will respond by cooing and gurgling. Later he will pick up a few words and sense the rhythm of language. Help him to add words to his <u>speaking vocabulary</u>. The more words he uses naturally in his ordinary conversation, the more words will have meaning for him when he sees them on the printed page.

2. <u>Listen</u> to your child.

   Children must have many opportunities to express themselves. Encourage your child to talk about things he has seen or done. The more the child talks, the better he is likely to read. Pay attention when he is talking with you. Listen to your child read. Suggest that before he reads aloud to you, he should read the story to himself to be sure he knows all the words. This makes listening to him read much more interesting to you.

3. <u>Read</u> to your child.

   Every time you read to him you are building an appreciation of books and reading. A child who has been read to is usually more anxious to read to himself. Reading becomes more important. Remember, his listening and interest levels are above his reading level.

4. <u>Help</u> him with his reading.

   Tell him the words if he's in the beginning stages of reading. Help him to work out the word if he's in a later stage by:
   (a) Looking at the picture,
   (b) Skipping over the unknown word and reading the rest of the sentence to see whether this suggests a new word,
   (c) Checking to see whether the word makes "sense" in the sentence.

5. <u>Teach</u> your child how to take care of books. He will then learn to regard books as friends.

6. <u>Take</u> him on trips.

   Even a short trip on the bus or subway will excite his curiosity and interest in the world around him. Point out interesting things and give him new words and meaning of words.

7. Build up a reading atmosphere at home.

    Have books, magazines, newspapers, etc. around the house. Let your child see you reading frequently. Tune in to worthwhile programs on the radio and television. Your child will tend to imitate his parents.

8. Encourage him to join the public library.

    Take him to the library at first. Don't tell him what books to select. If he is a poor reader, he may at first choose easy books. As he gains confidence, satisfaction, and improves in reading, he will choose more difficult books.

9. Buy games and puzzles for your child.

    These help your child learn shape and form and help him relate words to things. Anagrams, Letter Games, Scrabble, and Lotto will help him with his spelling and reading. Jigsaw puzzles help a child recognize shape because the puzzle piece must be matched to fit a space.

10. Make games.

    You can make simple word games by cutting words from a magazine and asking your child to match these words to a picture. Make word cards for troublesome words (was, there, what, went, etc.) and play a game with him. How quickly can he learn the word and how many word cards can be removed from the pack because he has really learned them? What words should be added?

11. Buy books for your child.

    For birthdays and holidays buy books when you can afford them. A child who owns a few good books is usually interested in reading. Try to get books at his reading grade level so he can read these books with fun and pleasure. Buy children's magazines too: Children's Digest, Humpty Dumpty, Calling All Girls, Boy's Life, etc.

12. Praise your child.

    Remember, reading is a difficult task. Don't forget to praise him when he succeeds. Don't expect him to know the word when you tell it once or twice or even ten or twenty times. Some normal children need to see a word many more times than this.

13. Keep your child well and rested.

    A child who has stayed up late to watch television shows the effect next day in his school work. Cooperate with the school nurse and doctor in correcting his vision or hearing or nutritional defects.

14. Give your child responsibilities which he is capable of taking.

    This allows him to earn recognition and to get real satisfaction from accomplishments.

15. See that your child has good habits of attendance.

    When he is absent from school, he misses his work and may not be able to keep up with his class.

16. <u>Check</u> your child's report card.
> If he is having trouble with reading or any subject consult his teacher to find out why and how you can help.

17. <u>Set aside</u> a regular time for homework.
> Give your child a definite place in which to work. Help him develop the habit of daily attention to homework routines.

18. <u>Guide</u> your child to the better movies, TV and radio programs.
> Select movies, radio and TV programs which will give him worthwhile information as well as entertainment. Check the newspaper listings for these programs.

19. <u>Accept</u> your child as he is.
> Don't compare him with his sister, brother or friend. Encourage him to improve as much as he can.

20. <u>Show</u> a real interest in school.
> The parents' attitude is usually the child's. You and the teacher are partners in the important job of teaching your child to read. An <u>interested, relaxed, helpful</u> parent is a most valuable co-worker, and <u>you</u> are the partners <u>we need</u>.

REMEMBER: Children learn to read by reading. The more they read, the better readers they become.

Yours truly,

_____

V. DiAngelo, Principal

Letter 1–90: READING HELP AT HOME

TO: Parents

Parents frequently want to know how they can help their child at home. The following suggestions have been used with positive results.

HOW A PARENT CAN HELP WITH READING AT HOME

1. Make your house a house of books; if you are a TV bug rather than a reader, your child is likely to be one, too.

2. Start with books that center around your child's interest-sports, airplanes, boats, construction kits, etc.

3. You did not get upset because the neighbor's child got a tooth before your child. Remember, reading skills are not all developed at the same time.

4. Introduce your child to the library. If the library is to be of lasting value to him, you must use it, too.

5. Give books as gifts for birthdays, Christmas, and so on.

6. Find a place in your home for your youngster to keep his books.

7. Do not send the child on an errand as soon as he sits down with a book.

8. Encourage your child to tell you about what he has read.

9. Find the time to discuss stories with him. Tell him about books you are reading.

10. Praise your child for his efforts. Compliment him on the progress made and not necessarily on the level reached.

11. Encourage your child to share his knowledge of reading with a younger child. Nothing will turn a youngster on more to reading than assuming the role of reading teacher.

12. Subscribe to a children's magazine. There are many good ones available today. Your child will look forward to his own mail and reading material.

13. Supply words your child does not know when he reads to you. Do this objectively without any comment. Do not appear annoyed if he stumbles on a word you helped him with before.

14. If you feel you must drill your child on certain words, make simple flash cards out of paper. Reward him for words he masters. Show him concrete examples of his "learning" by enumerating the words he knows. Have him tear up the word cards he no longer needs.

15. Enjoy the process. Let your child know that you do not mind helping him. Don't make your child feel that reading with him is painful for you.

Letter 1–91: READING TEST PERFORMANCE

March 14, 19XX
RE: Barbara Caputo
CLASS: 6A

Dear Mrs. Caputo:

Congratulations! We have just received the results of this year's reading test and your child achieved in the 99th percentile. This means that your child scored in the top 1 percent of the country on the <u>total</u> reading test. This is really something to be proud of!

Your child's teacher shares my pride and deserves much of the credit, as do you the parent of such an outstanding pupil.

I'm sure there will be many occasions in the future when Barbara will bring you joy and a sense of achievement. I did not want this precursor of honors to come to go unnoticed.

Best wishes for continued success.

Sincerely,

_____

V. DiAngelo, Principal

Letter 1–92: UNDERSTANDING READING TEST SCORES

Dear Parents,

Teachers, guidance counselors, and school administrators are tremendously interested in their students' reading test scores. These tests are designed to measure how well a child reads compared to other children in the same grade. Many schools actually place a greater importance on a child's reading test scores than on report card marks to determine class placement.

Reading test results are easy to understand. Children's scores are usually given in grade equivalents. Suppose a child scores 6.3 ("six point three") on a reading test. These numbers mean that the child reads as well as an "average" child in the third month of the sixth grade. (The first number shows the child's grade ability, while the second number indicates the month of that school year).

Let's look at some sample scores in the same way a school would. Here are three children's test scores for the past two years:

	test scores in 6th grade	test scores in 7th grade
Mark	6.2	8.5
Jennifer	6.7	7.8
Susan	4.6	4.9

Schools expect that a student's reading ability will go up at least one year in a year's time. Of our three students, Mark has clearly made the greatest reading progress over the past year. He has improved from 6.2 (sixth grade, second month) to 8.5 (eighth grade, fifth month). These scores represent an improvement of 2.3 years ability (or two years, three months) in only one year's time ($8.5 - 6.2 = 2.3$).

Jennifer has improved 1.1 years over the past year ($7.8 - 6.7 = 1.1$).

Susan shows the least improvement. Her reading score has increased only .3 years (or three months) since the last test ($4.9 - 4.6 = .3$).

Mark and Jennifer show satisfactory improvement in reading ability over the past year. Susan's score, however, shows that she is falling behind in reading ability.

Sincerely,

_____

V. DiAngelo, Principal

Letter 1–93: REMEDIAL HELP

January 10, 19XX
RE: Joey Price
CLASS: 4B

Dear Mr. and Mrs. Price:

As you know from the last report card and from our conference, your son, Joey, has had a great deal of difficulty with work in mathematics.

His teacher, Mr. Corbett, has given Joey special attention in class and has met with him after school in an effort to provide individual help. Progress has been slow. I am convinced that Joey needs remedial/tutorial help. We do have a peer tutoring service in school. This is provided at no cost to the parents. Pupils must report before school each day to receive this tutoring.

It will be necessary for you to make the transportation arrangements. If, for any reason, you would rather arrange for private tutoring I hope you will do so promptly. By providing the needed help now, we can still hope to see Joey pass grade 4 before the end of the term.

Please call me at school to tell me of your wish in this matter.

Sincerely,

_____

V. DiAngelo, Principal

Letter 1–94: REQUEST FOR CLINICAL SERVICE

February 5, 19XX
RE: Grace Haussmann
Class: 3A

Dear Mr. and Mrs. Haussmann:

We are fortunate to have the services of a social worker/psychologist at our school. Such professionals together with parents and teachers have been quite successful in helping many of our pupils make a better adjustment to school.

Your daughter Grace has been referred to our social worker/psychologist for evaluation. This interview will be kept strictly confidential. As soon as Dr. Gligor has finished his report, you will be contacted so that the findings can be shared with you. No notation will be made on your child's permanent record. No further counseling will be offered unless you give your permission in writing.

At this time we are merely asking that you give your approval for the initial evaluation. Please give a phone number where we can reach you to arrange for a confidential report when this first contact is completed.

Yours truly,

_____

V. DiAngelo, Principal

----------------------- DETACH AND RETURN TO SCHOOL -----------------------

Dear Principal:

I give permission to have my child _____ seen by the school social worker/psychologist.

Comments: _____

_____

_____

Parent's Signature   Date

Letter 1-95: RESPONSE TO PARENT'S LETTER

April 11, 19XX
RE: Jerry Newberg
Class: 7C

Dear Mr. and Mrs. Newberg:

I have received your letter dated April 8 regarding your child. In reviewing the contents of your letter I realize that you have made some specific points that I would like to discuss with you.

The opinions of parents like yourself are very important to me. I would like to review your complaint with you directly. Please call me at 761-5511 for an appointment to come to school so that together we can review the contents of your letter. If it is easier for you to discuss this matter over the telephone, please let me know a convenient time when I can call you. Perhaps I can call you some evening; or, I will be most happy to receive your call at school.

Yours truly,

_____

V. DiAngelo, Principal

Letter 1–96: RESPONSE TO PARENT'S LETTER

November 19, 19XX
RE: Sally Cartwright
Class: 3B

Dear Mr. Cartwright:

Thank you for your letter dated November 15 in which you ask for information regarding:

_____ Registration

_____ Homework

_____ Promotion Standards

_____ Report Cards

_____ Absence/Lateness

_____ Textbooks

_____ Discipline

_____ Lunch

_____ Transportation

We encourage parent involvement in the education of their children. I am enclosing a copy of our school policy on the matter you brought up.

If you would like more information or if you have any questions, please phone me at 761-5511.

I look forward to meeting with you at the next PTA meeting which will be held on December 8 at 7:30 P.M.

Yours truly,

_____

V. DiAngelo, Principal

Letter 1–97:   SAFETY

TO: Parents
RE: Safety to and from Schools

  Safety is important. Children should be encouraged to practice good safety habits. Safety instruction is given at school and safety measures are practiced in the building and on the playground. You can help your child develop good safety habits by providing safety instruction at home.

If your child is new at school,

1. Assist him/her in learning the safest route to and from school.

2. Encourage him/her to use intersections when crossing a street rather than the middle of the block. Where crosswalks are provided, he/she should stay between the lines. It is the child's responsibility to make certain that traffic from both directions has stopped.

3. If there are no sidewalks, the child should walk on the left side of the street facing oncoming traffic.

4. Encourage him/her to come home immediately after school. Discourage any stops along the way home.

5. He/she should obey traffic lights and look both ways before crossing a street.

6. Remind your child to:

  a. Never accept rides or gifts from strangers.

  b. Report to his/her teacher, a police officer, his/her bus driver, or to you any strangers seen loitering on foot or in a car near schools, playgrounds, etc.

  c. Always try to secure the license number of the car and write it down.

  d. Always try to remember what the stranger looked like and how he was dressed.

  e. Contact a police officer any time he/she needs help.

7. Kindergarten: For those kindergarten children riding the buses at least for the first 3 days of school it is important that a name tag be attached to the child's clothing.

8. When a child is to go home with another child or to be left at another stop, there should be a notice from home.

Letter 1–98: SCIENCE

Dear Parents:

There are many ways you can help your child improve his background in science. Here are some suggestions:

1. For birthdays and at Christmastime give gifts such as science kits, weather instruments, telescopes, microscopes, nature and science books, etc.

2. Take nature vacations or excursions. Examine natural surroundings, trees, rocks, earth formations, animals, insects, etc. Help your child to classify some of these.

3. Make use of our valuable community and city resources such as:

   Planetarium
   Museums
   Wildlife Refuges
   Space Centers
   Zoos
   Aquarium
   Botanical Gardens
   Computer Centers

4. Encourage your children to watch worthwhile science and nature television shows. Before each program try to anticipate together what may be presented. After the program sum up together what has been learned, and then evaluate the program.

5. Encourage interest in science fair projects. Help your youngster to decide on a project, to secure needed materials, and to evalute his completed project. Leave the actual planning and doing to him!
   (NOTE: This year our science fair will be held on Tuesday, February 5, in the school gym.)

6. Help your child to start a science library. This could include files of interesting science articles saved from newspapers and magazines.

Yours truly,

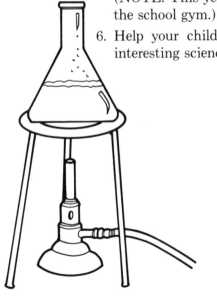

_____

V. DiAngelo, Principal

Letter 1–99:   SEX EDUCATION

Dear Parents,

At this time your child will begin instruction in Sex Education. In our present-day society it is necessary for children to develop the personal and social competence that leads to individual fulfillment and social progress. One of the areas of study which is essential in developing these competencies is the area of family living, including sex education. While family structures within our society vary, every person shares the common characteristic of membership in a family.

The major responsibility for the formation of attitudes conducive to wholesome development rests with the home. Religious institutions, the school, and other organizations have supplementary roles in providing children with the basis for making valid moral and ethical judgements. The schools have the resources to provide a comprehensive, sequential, up-to-date program which will assist children in developing respect, restraint, and a sense of responsibility for their own lives and the lives of others. The program we offer has been carefully worked out by the Central School District and this school.

Sincerely,

_____

V. DiAngelo, Principal

---------------------- Please sign and return to your child's teacher ----------------------

_____

Date

Dear Principal:

_____ I give my permission for my son/daughter to receive instruction in Sex Education.

_____ I do not give my permission for my son/daughter to receive instruction in Sex Education.

_____

Parent's Signature

_____   _____

Child's Name   Class

Letter 1–100: SOCIAL STUDIES

Dear Parent:

Years ago the emphasis in social studies was on simply learning isolated facts; today it's on the development of concepts and understandings that can be applied to new situations, and on the development of critical thinking skills.

The goals of the social studies program include developing an understanding of how man interacts with his environment, what he has learned from the past, and how what he does today affects his future.

Listed below are some ways you can help your child in the area of social studies:

1. Make "Let's look it up" an important phrase in your household.

2. Have good reference material on hand—e.g., an Atlas, a globe, an almanac, and, if possible, an encyclopedia and past issues of magazines such as the National Geographic.

3. Regularly get at least one good newspaper and news magazine.

4. Tune in often to a variety of TV and radio news and current affairs programs.

5. Try to make interesting news of the day part of dinner table conversation. Give your child a chance to express his views.

6. Let your child have a large world map on the wall of his room so that he can use it for ready reference in connection with current events.

7. Encourage the development of a worthwhile hobby—e.g., collecting stamps, flags, travel posters, dolls in native costumes, postcards, foreign coins, etc.

8. Explore the local area with him—points of historical interest, shopping centers and markets, museums, docks, factories, radio and TV stations, etc.

9. Take your child on trips whenever possible. Visit interesting places and encourage him to jot down impressions of what he sees.

10. Help your child to judge people as individuals and not as members of racial or religious groups.

Yours truly,

_____

V. DiAngelo, Principal

Letter 1–101: SPELLING BEE

April 10, 19XX

Dear Mr. and Mrs. Wade:

   I am delighted to inform you that your daughter, Randi, was a finalist in our school Spelling Bee. This is quite an achievement! The competition was very close. Your daughter showed great poise as well as skill in defeating the twenty-five other class champions.
   Randi is a credit to her school and, of course, her home. We are proud to see the positive results of your training and our instruction.
   I hope the future will bring many more honors and successes to Randi. I am sure this is just the beginning.

Sincerely yours,

_____

V. DiAngelo, Principal

Letter 1–102: SPORTS PARTICIPATION PERMISSION

September 30, 19XX
RE: Keith Paige
Class: 6A

Dear Mr. and Mrs. Paige:

We would like to include your son/daughter in our volleyball program. We need your signed permission as well as the following data:

Any serious accidents or injuries? If yes, explain. _____

_____

Surgical Operations: _____

_____

Allergies: _____

Hernia: _____ Diabetes: _____

Vision: _____ Hearing: _____

Cardiac: _____ Orthopedic: _____

Present Medication: _____ Reason: _____

Any previous rejection from competitive sports (date and reason): _____

_____

The answers to the above are correct. I understand that by giving my permission I shall assume all responsibility for any injury received in practice or participation.

_____   _____
Date   Parent's Signature

Letter 1–103: SUSPENSION

January 21, 19XX
RE: Mike Gleason
Class: 5B

Dear Mr. and Mrs. Gleason:

I regret to inform you that it has become necessary to suspend your child from school. This has become necessary because of several incidents. The precipitating

cause for this suspension occurred on January 15. On that date your son _____

_____

_____

_____

_____

The suspension will begin on January 26, 19XX and last through February 3, 19XX. Mike may return to school on February 6. During this period of suspension, your child must be kept at home during school hours.

I am most anxious to meet with you so that we can work out a plan together that will help Mike adjust to school life, and learn to observe some basic rules of safety and order. I hope that you can come to my office on January 25 at 4 P.M. If, for any reason, this day or time is not convenient, please call me at 761-5511 and I will be happy to change the appointment. If you wish to bring someone with you who can help us achieve our mutual goal, please let me know.

Sincerely,

_____

V. DiAngelo, Principal

cc: District Supt.
    Guidance File

Letter 1–104: THANK YOU

March 11, 19XX

Dear Mrs. Hines:

Please accept my compliments on a difficult job well done! When you undertook the Chinese Auction (a first for P.S. 54) I looked at you with mixed feelings of admiration and sympathy. I admired your courage at attempting such a Herculean task. I also felt sympathetic since this had not been done here before and because the ever-successful bazaars would be a tough act to follow.

Your determination, optimism, and organizational ability made last Friday's Chinese Auction the event of the decade. It attracted more people and made more money than any previous fund raiser. I marvelled at the quiet, efficient manner in which you went about your business. You were never ruffled and never lost your "cool." All this in spite of a snowstorm, alternate date, and all the other frustrations that accompany an undertaking of this magnitude. Your ability in planning, delegating, and checking made this event the great success it was.

On behalf of our 700 students I thank you for your tireless efforts on their behalf. What a wonderful example you set for your own children and others in the area of community and school service!

Sincerely,

_____

V. DiAngelo, Principal

Letter 1–105: THANK YOU

December 12, 19XX

Dear Mr. Campbell:

Thank you for your letter dated December 7 in which you paid our school a compliment. Your well-worded letter is most welcome. While we frequently get notes of praise from grateful parents, I was particularly impressed with your letter in which you

listed such specific items as ⸺⸺⸺⸺⸺⸺⸺⸺⸺⸺⸺⸺

⸺⸺⸺⸺⸺⸺⸺⸺⸺⸺⸺⸺⸺⸺⸺⸺

I took the liberty of showing your letter to those staff members who have directly contributed to your son's smooth adjustment to our school.

How nice of you to take time from your busy schedule to send us that gratifying message. No wonder your son, Thomas, has such a pleasing personality. If we can ever be of any assistance to you or any of your family, please do not hesitate to ask.

Sincerely,

⸺⸺⸺⸺⸺⸺⸺⸺⸺⸺⸺⸺

V. DiAngelo, Principal

Letter 1–106: THANK YOU TO RETIRING PTA LEADER

June 8, 19XX

Dear Mrs. Schultz:

It is with sadness that I note the end of your two years as PTA President. Working with you during this exciting period in our school history has been extremely fruitful and pleasant.

The various cooperative efforts of the P.T.A. and school administration have been mutually rewarding. Many projects such as the After-School Enrichment Center could not have come about without your help and encouragement.

I have been continually impressed with your insight into school problems, your ability to deal with a variety of people, and your eternal optimism.

Good luck to you and your son, Harry, as he begins Franklin Heights High School in the Fall.

Sincerely,

_____

V. DiAngelo, Principal

Letter 1–107: THANK YOU

December 3, 19XX

Dear Mr. and Mrs. Monroe:

Thank you for the complimentary letter that arrived here on a cold, dark Monday morning. Your effusive praise is most appreciated and I have conveyed your sentiments to the teachers involved, Mrs. Hoogerhyde and Mrs. Zimmerman. May I assure you that the commendable qualities you mentioned are also recognized by the school administration at P.S. 54.

Both your sons, Allen and Jeff, are welcome additions to our school. We are delighted to have them with us. I am reminded of the adage: "The apple doesn't fall far from the tree," and so look forward to meeting you.

Sincerely,

_____

V. DiAngelo, Principal

Letter 1–108: TRIP CONSENT FORM

Date _____

Dear Parents,

Your child _____ of class _____ is invit-

ed to participate in a class trip to _____

_____

on _____. The class will leave at _____ and

return at _____. Have your child bring a bag lunch. The cost of the

trip includes _____. The money will be

collected from _____ to _____. Your child may

bring some spending money for the trip. Please do not give your child more than

_____ to spend.

We are interested in having some parents with us on the trip to help supervise

the students. If you are able to accompany the class on _____,
please check the box below.

Whether or not you will accompany us, please sign the tear-off slip below to
give your child permission to go on the trip. Keep this top half to remind yourself of the
date and the site of the trip.

Sincerely,

_____

V. DiAngelo, Principal

------------------------------------ (tear off and return) ------------------------------------

I give my child _____ of class _____

permission to attend the class trip on _____
☐ I will be able to accompany the class.
☐ I will not be able to accompany the class.

_____

Parent's Signature

Letter 1–109: TRUANCY

May 2, 19XX
RE: Jeremy Sanderson
Class: 7A

Dear Mr. and Mrs. Sanderson:

We believe that your son, Jeremy, was absent from school without your permission on April 30. Since your child did not come to school that day and did not bring a note on the following day, we have marked him "truant."

Academic success is dependent on continuous attendance. It is the parent's responsibility to ensure that the youngster is in daily attendance.

I am bringing this matter to your attention now so that you can impress your child with the importance of school and the obligation to attend school every day.

Sincerely,

_____

V. DiAngelo, Principal

-------------------------------- Please detach and return ----------------------------------

Dear Principal:

I have spoken to _____ of Class _____

about your letter describing nonattendance on _____, 19____.

Comments: _____

_____

_____

Parent's Signature

Letter 1–110: VIOLATION OF SCHOOL RULES

November 24, 19XX
RE: Charlie MacGregor
CLASS: 3A

Dear Mr. and Mrs. MacGregor:

Your child, Charlie, has usually behaved well in school. In the last few days, however, he has broken several school rules. His teacher, Ms. Buckner, has referred Charlie to me. I have spoken to your son and have received a promise to improve. If there is no improvement, I shall be obliged to ask you to come to school. This will be for a pre-suspension conference. I am confident that with your help, we will be able to avoid this step.

Your son has already been told the specific violations involved. I am listing some of them below. Please discuss these with your child with a view toward bringing about an improvement.

Sincerely,

_____
V. DiAngelo, Principal

Specific violations of school rules: _____

_____

_____

_____

_____

_____

_____

V.I.P.
VERY IMPORTANT PARENT

P.S. 54 salutes
the many contributions of

_____

to the students and staff
at our school.

_____   _____

Date   Principal

Letter 1–112: VOLUNTEERS

TO: Parents

The P.T.A. of P.S. 54 once again needs the support of all parents. If you would like to help in any of the areas listed below, please indicate your choice and interests and return this form to your child's homeroom teacher. Please consider participating in some way. The P.T.A. needs your help!

1. Trip Escorts (Parents to accompany class excursions) (   )
2. Library (One hour per week: 2:15-3:00 P.M.) (   )
3. Publicity (Newspaper articles, posters, etc.) (   )
4. Nurse's Office (Two hours per week typing and/or clerical) (   )
5. Tutoring (As a helper or aide to a Department Head) (   )
   A. Math (   )   B. Reading (   )
6. Refreshments (Baking for school functions) (   )
7. P.T.A. Newsletter (To help with typing, etc.) (   )
8. Telephone (Occasional phoning if necessary) (   )
9. Pep Club (To help promote school spirit) (   )
10. Other (All time, talents, and ideas welcome) (   )

NAME: _____

TELEPHONE NUMBER: _____

GRADE OF CHILD IN SCHOOL: _____

COMMENTS: _____

_____

_____

_____

Letter 1–113: WEEKLY LETTER TO PARENTS

February 27, 19XX

Dear Parents:

There are just a few items of interest this week. First, our enrollment appears to be gradually creeping upwards. We have picked up about 15 to 20 students in the past couple of weeks. From the information I can gather, I suspect we will have slow but steady growth the rest of this year and the next, and then we will begin to grow rather rapidly. At this time there are approximately 300 living units under construction in the school community. It is difficult to say when these will be completed or exactly how many youngsters we will get from them.

On Tuesday evening at 7:30, the Parent Advisory Committee is sponsoring a reading workshop for parents. This workshop will be led by Miss Martin, one of our two very able reading teachers. We will meet in the library. Any interested parent is invited to attend. Please notify the office so we will know you are coming.

We have a very exciting cultural arts program coming up Wednesday morning of next week. Craig McKay, a mime, will present a show at 9:30 for the kindergarten through third grades and at approximately 10:10 for the upper grades. Mr. McKay will also be doing a program on March 24 for our next P.T.A. meeting.

I have one concern with which I would like you to help us. Each morning it seems to me as if more children are being left off at school very early. School really does not begin until 9:00, and except for very bad weather conditions, the youngsters are not allowed in the building until 8:45. The early morning time from 8:30 to 9:00 is planning time for the teachers and, as a consequence, children who are here very early may not be supervised. We are not even expected to report to work officially until 8:30; however, those of us who come in early notice that there are many children already here—a few even as early as 7:30. I would ask your cooperation in not dropping your children off at school before 8:45 unless they are here for a very specific educational reason such as for tutoring by a teacher.

Have a nice weekend.

Sincerely Yours,

_____

V. DiAngelo, Principal

SECTION
2

Letters
to
Students

Letter 2–1: ACADEMIC CONTRACT

I, _____, of Class _____, agree to follow the rules checked below as part of my contract. I understand that the terms of this

contract will be in effect until June _____. If the rules are violated, the contract will be considered broken and I may be kept from promotion, graduation, or other rewards.

At the end of each Marking Period this contract will be reviewed. If I meet the terms of this contract it will be considered fulfilled and returned to me.

_____ 1. Attend all classes promptly.

_____ 2. Hand in all homework assignments on time.

_____ 3. Do all written work neatly.

_____ 4. Come to school with all necessary books and supplies.

_____ 5. Improve scores on tests and quizzes.

_____ 6. Participate in class discussions.

_____ 7. Speak clearly when called upon.

I have read the above Academic Contract and agree to meet the terms as stated.

Date: _____ Pupil's Name: _____ Class: _____

Pupil's Signature: _____

Parent's Signature: _____

Teacher's Signature: _____

Letter 2–2: PUPIL ACTIVITY SURVEY

Name: _____ Class: _____ Date: _____

Activity: _____

Dear Student:

  We would like to have your reaction to the activity listed above. Please take a moment to read each of these questions carefully. We would like your honest response to each question. These survey forms will help us provide the kinds of activities that best meet your needs.

       Thank you.

       _____

       V. DiAngelo, Principal

****

1. While engaged in this activity how did you feel about . . .

  (a) what you were doing? _____

  (b) yourself? _____

  (c) the faculty adviser? _____

  (d) your classmates? _____

2. What do you think your faculty adviser's feelings were about the activity?

  _____

  _____

  _____

3. Would you recommend some other staff member for this activity? Why?

  _____

  _____

  _____

4. What part of this activity did you like best?

_____

_____

_____

5. What part didn't you like?

_____

_____

_____

6. How did you feel when the activity was over?

_____

_____

_____

7. If you could change the activity, what would you recommend?

_____

_____

_____

8. Do you have any other comments you care to share? What are they?

_____

_____

_____

_____

_____

Letter 2-3: BEHAVIOR CONTRACT

I, _____, of Class _____, on this day: _____, 19____, promise to follow the terms of this contract as checked below:

I <u>will</u>:

____ raise my hand before speaking   ____ keep my desk neat and clean

____ stay in my seat   ____ come prepared to work

____ stand in place on line

____ _____

____ _____

I will NOT:

____ call out answers   ____ chew gum or candy in class

____ crack jokes in class   ____ annoy other pupils

____ write on the covers of my books   ____ interrupt the class

____ _____

____ _____

Every Friday my teacher, _____, will review this contract with me at a conference. If I improve, it will be renewed. If I do not improve, I may have my class changed.

In addition, _____

_____

SEAL

Pupil's Signature: _____

Parent's Signature: _____

Teacher's Signature: _____

COMMENDATION ☆ ☆

_____
(School)

commends _____

of class _____ for

_____

_____

on this _____ day of _____, 19____

_____
Principal

Letter 2–5: CONSERVING SCHOOL SUPPLIES

November 7, 19XX

TO: ALL PUPILS
FROM: V. DiAngelo, Principal
RE: CONSERVING SCHOOL SUPPLIES

We need your help. Each pupil in our school can be part of the solution to a big school problem—waste. Many of the school supplies you need are being wasted. We all know how important money is. Money taken from your parents' taxes buys the paper, pencils, books, and supplies that you use in school.

You can help us by making sure that none of these supplies are wasted. Do not use two sheets of paper when one will do. Keep you books in good condition by covering them. Take only the materials you need to do the job. Your parents conserve energy at home and your job is to help conserve materials here at school. If you see other pupils wasting school supplies, ask them to stop.

I am depending on all of you to help prevent waste and conserve our school supplies.

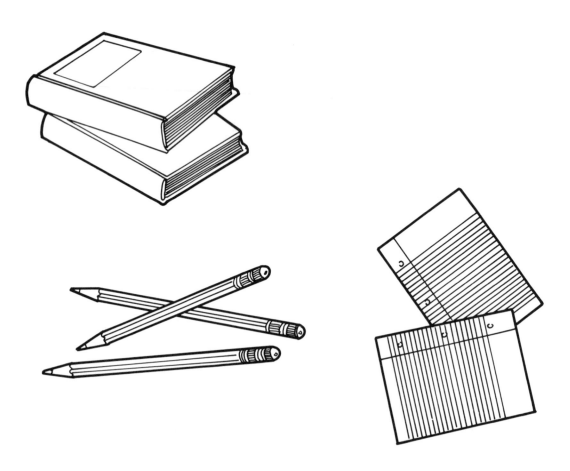

Letter 2-6: DANCE RULES

TO: ALL EIGHTH GRADE STUDENTS
RE: SCHOOL DANCE RULES

All students at P.S. 54 are expected to conduct themselves properly at all times. One of the most popular eighth grade activities is the May Spring Dance. While 99 percent of the students behave properly, we will not allow a few unruly students to spoil this activity for the majority of our eighth grade class who have the right to enjoy the activity. Please read these rules which have been drawn up by a committee made up of your fellow classmates, some staff members, and two parents from our P.T.A.

After you have read these rules, we would welcome any comments you may have. A space has been provided for your reaction. Please place the lower half of this notice in my office. You need not sign your name.

Sincerely,

_____

V. DiAngelo, Principal

DANCE RULES

1. Only students with a ticket will be admitted to the dance.
2. Once a student leaves the dance, he or she may not be readmitted.
3. All school and state laws regarding alcohol and other substances are in effect.
4. Proper school conduct is required at all times.
5. The dress code drawn up for the particular dance must be observed.
6. Dances held at the school will be chaperoned by teachers and the school security guard.
7. Students from other schools may not attend school dances held on campus.
8. Organizations planning a dance must notify the office at least two weeks in advance.
9. Students must show their I.D. cards for school-sponsored dances.
10. All dances must end by 1 A.M.

--------------- DETACH AND RETURN TO PRINCIPAL'S OFFICE ----------------

COMMENTS _____

_____

_____

Signature _____ Homeroom _____

Letter 2–7: DETENTION

DETENTION NOTICE

TO: _____ of Class: _____ Date: _____

    You have been assigned detention by _____ for the reason(s) checked below. Please report for detention on _____ at ____ o'clock. You will be in the detention room for ____ minutes. The detention room is

_____.

    It is your responsibility to tell your parents 24 hours in advance of the date you will be staying after school. Have them sign below and return this notice to

_____.

____ Sloppy or incomplete school work

____ Inattention or disruption in class

____ Coming to school without materials

____ Rudeness in talking to adults in school

____ Continued lateness

____ Other: _____

_____
                    Principal

_____

Pupil's Signature   Class   Parent's Signature   Date

Letter 2–8: DETENTION

TO: Students
RE: Pupil Detention

     Over 90 percent of our students have never received a detention notice in their entire school career. For those few pupils who insist upon breaking school rules we have established a detention room after school.
     Our rules for detention are simple:

1. Students are given a minimum of 24 hours notice before being asked to serve detention.

2. Bus students may use this time to arrange alternate transportation.

3. Students who participate in afterschool activities can avoid detention by simply obeying the school rules. Participation in sports or other afterschool activities is not a substitute for detention.

4. Students wishing to see a teacher after school for remedial help may do so. This takes priority over but is not a substitute for detention. The helping teacher must write a note for the student to give to the assistant principal verifying the extra help session. Detention is then postponed for one day.

5. Students serving detention must report to the detention room promptly. Any student not in his seat five minutes after the close of school is considered late and must serve one additional day.

_____ I have read the rules for Pupil Detention and understand them.

_____ I have read the rules for Pupil Detention and have the following question:

_____

_____

Pupils's Name: _____

Class: _____   Date: _____

Letter 2-9: DRESS CODE FOR LOWER GRADES

TO: All Pupils in Grades 1-6
FR: V. DiAngelo, Principal
RE: Dress Code

At P.S. 54, we are proud of the way our pupils look when they come to school. We feel that you and your parents have the right to choose clothing based upon your own sense of taste and style. The same applies to hair and grooming.

We do insist on the following rules:

1. Clothes or hair must not present a danger to the health and safety of the student or other students.
2. Appearance must not cause an interference with school work or create classroom disorder.
3. Students and their clothing must be neat and clean.

Thank you for your cooperation. Please take this notice home. Go over it with your parent(s). Sign the "tear-off" below along with your parent. Bring the signed portion to your teacher.

Sincerely,

_____

V. DiAngelo, Principal

Dear Principal:

I have read the notice on School Dress.

_____

Parent's Signature   Pupil's Name   Date

Letter 2-10: DRESS CODE FOR UPPER GRADES

TO: All Pupils
FR: V. DiAngelo, Principal
RE: Dress Code

At P.S. 54, we take pride in the appearance of our students. The way you look reflects your attitude towards school and yourself. All students are expected to dress and groom themselves neatly and appropriately.

A clean, neat appearance is primary. The only restrictions we have were developed at a meeting with pupil, parent, and teacher representatives. Dress that tends to disrupt the class or contribute to a safety hazard will result in a phone call to your parents asking that they bring a change of clothing.

Among the "no-no's" for school are:

1. T-shirts with obscene or vulgar messages
2. Bare feet
3. Dangling earrings for boys
4. Inappropriate makeup
5. Revealing or provocative clothing

Your cooperation in raising the image of the school as well as your own is appreciated.

If you have any comment on this memo, please write it down on the coupon below and place it in my letter box outside the Office. Thank you.

Dear

I have read your memo about pupil dress and would like to suggest that ____

_____

_____

_____

_____

Pupil's Name (Optional)

Letter 2–11: EVALUATION OF SCHOOL ACTIVITIES

TO: Students

      Please read each statement about School Activities. If you feel they rate very high place a "5" in the column. If you feel our school ranks very low in this area, write in a "1". You may use any numbers in between. Remember, it's your choice that counts.

1. Our school has a wide variety of student activities.	1.
2. There is a balance of during-school and after-school activities.	2.
3. Students have a say in the kinds of activities offered.	3.
4. There is a balance between athletics and other activities.	4.
5. When activities are offered, I am able to get my first choice.	5.
6. Girls as well as boys are encouraged to join activities.	6.
7. Pupils from different groups are made welcome.	7.
8. We have sufficient equipment for our activities.	8.
9. Pupil suggestions are taken seriously.	9.

10. If you could, what would you do to improve the activities at our school?

_____

_____

_____

_____

_____

Thank you!

_____

Principal

Letter 2–12: FIELD DAY

May 25, 19XX

ATTENTION: Pupils in Grades 3, 4, and 5

Field Day is almost here!

                          Tuesday, June 8 – all 3rd Grade Classes
                          Wednesday, June 9 – all 4th Grade Classes
                          Thursday, June 10 – all 5th Grade Classes

Place: Lindsay Field
Rain Date: Same day in school gym.

Events: Relay races, sack race, three-legged race, balloon bust, broad jump, dashes, softball throw, and more.

Wear play clothes, bring something to sit on and wholesome treats to munch.

Leave school, on foot, at 9:00 A.M.
Arrive at Lindsay Field at 9:30 A.M.
Return at 11:30 A.M. Lunch at school.

Parent help will be most welcome. Volunteers should contact their child's teacher.

I'll see you at the Field Day events!

_____

V. DiAngelo, Principal

To _____

For _____

_____

_____

_____

_____

Principal

_____

Date

Letter 2–14: INTRODUCTION TO PUPIL HANDBOOK

Welcome to P.S. 54 and to the new and exciting adventures and experiences that await you here. The amount of time and effort you give will make your stay here happy and memorable.

We have prepared this handbook to tell you about our school. You will find that the rules and regulations that govern our lives here at P.S. 54 make it possible for all of us to live, learn, work, and play together.

Take the time to read this book carefully. Don't put it off. Be sure you understand everything in it. Have your parents read it too. If you have any questions about anything, see your teachers, advisors, guidance counselors, administrators, or other staff members. They will be glad to answer your questions.

P.S. 54 will be whatever you make it. Be proud of it. Take good care of it. Become part of it. You have the power to determine your successes or failures. Start off on the right foot. Remember, the longest journey starts with just a single step. Put your best foot forward.

Good luck!

_____

V. DiAngelo, Principal

Happy Birthday

IMPORTANT INFORMATION ON:

_____

Birthday and Year _____   Place of Birth _____

Height on Birthday _____   Weight on Birthday _____

Number of Brothers _____ Names _____

Number of Sisters _____ Names _____

Pets _____

Favorites: TV Show _____

Recess Game _____   Snack Food _____

School Subject _____   Book _____

Kind of Music _____   Holiday _____

Sport _____   Audio Tape _____

Video Tape _____   Male Singer _____

Female Singer _____   Movie _____

Color _____   Main Dish Food _____

Beverage _____   Ice Cream Flavor _____

Cake _____   Flower _____

Happy Thought: _____

_____

of Class _____

is recognized for

_____

_____

_____

Principal

_____

Date

Letter 2–17: HONOR ROLL

To: Brad Collins   Class: 5B   Date: February 6, 19XX

Dear Brad:

I am happy to see that you have earned a place on our school Honor Roll for the second marking period. Congratulations on this outstanding achievement!

We at P.S. 54 are very proud of the students who are named to the Honor Roll. It signifies not only attributes of high scholarship, character, and service but also the admiration of your fellow students and teachers.

Your parents, I am sure, share my pride in your academic performance. This will be just a first step toward future high attainment and self-fulfillment. I am so glad that you are part of our school.

Good luck!

Sincerely,

_____

V. DiAngelo, Principal

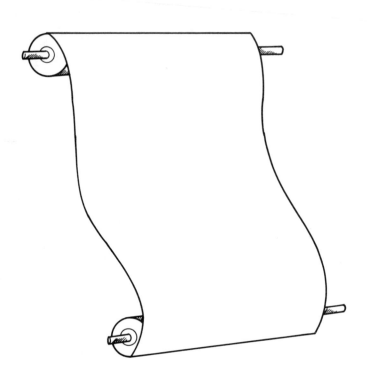

Letter 2–18: LOCKERS

TO: ALL PUPILS
FR: V. DiAngelo, Principal
RE: Lockers

At P.S. 54 we respect the privacy of each pupil and provide hall and gym lockers for the storing of clothing, school supplies, and other personal property. We also realize that a locker may occasionally be used to store items that are illegal or dangerous to others.

Under the law these lockers are the property of the Board of Education. They may be inspected to protect the school from harm. The school will cooperate with state and federal authorities after protecting the rights of the pupil involved.

Pupils are reminded NOT to hold or store packages for a friend. If any unlawful material is found in your locker, it will be assumed that you put it there.

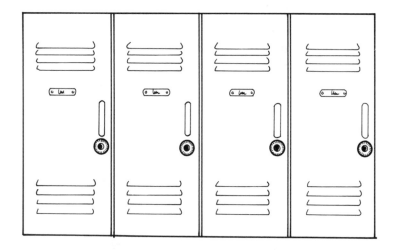

Letter 2-19: LUNCHROOM

TO: ALL STUDENTS

In order to make the lunch period as pleasant as possible, we need your help. As you know, our lunchroom is crowded and sometimes noisy. After meeting with some pupils, parents, and teachers, we have come up with these simple rules. We need everyone's cooperation to make our lunchroom a pleasant place to be. Please read these rules now.

1. Be seated as soon as you enter the lunchroom.
2. Talk to your neighbor quietly. Do not call out to students at other tables.
3. When your table is called, line up at the steam table.
4. Carry your tray carefully back to your seat.
5. Eat your food in a well-mannered way. Do not talk while eating.
6. Never throw food or drop food or paper on the floor.
7. Clean up your own eating area by putting refuse on your empty tray.
8. When you are told to do so, deposit all refuse in the trash cans.
9. Proceed to the recess area without running or shouting.
10. All other school rules apply during the lunch period.

If you have any suggestions as to how we can improve the lunch period, please write them on the back of this letter and drop it off at the office.

Thank you for your cooperation.

_____

V. DiAngelo, Principal

Letter 2–20:   MATH TEST

TO: ALL PUPILS
RE: TAKING A MATH TEST

Avoiding careless errors:
1. Be sure your answer is reasonable.

2. Work neatly. It fosters accuracy.

3. Organization is important. It helps reduce errors.

4. If time permits, recheck your work. Use scrap paper.

5. Reread each question after you have completed your work to be certain you have answered the particular question.

6. Do not write over numbers. Rewrite numbers when changes occur.

Reducing nervousness:
1. Start reviewing far enough in advance.

2. Study small chunks of material rather than the whole term's work at each of your study sessions.

3. Have confidence in your ability. Nobody has a complete math "block."

4. Don't worry to the point of anxiety.

5. Do the questions that you are sure of first.

6. Get a good night's rest the night before the test.

Making the most of the allotted time:
1. Look over the whole test quickly and do the problems you are sure of first.

2. Give thought to a common-sense approach to the solution as well as formulas.

3. Construct drawings or charts that can improve your "picture" of the problem.

4. Estimate your answer before beginning work.

5. Check your work for careless errors in computation.

Letter 2–21: METRICS

TO: MATH PUPILS
RE: METRIC MEASURING LICENSE

This letter will entitle you to be an OFFICIAL METRIC MEASURER, authorized to measure, at any time, using metric units (cm, dm, m, km, g, or kg) anything that can be measured, either with measuring tools or by estimation.

Pupil's Name: _____ Class: _____ Date: _____

Height _____cm   Palm width _____cm   Thumb _____cm

Index finger _____cm   Ring finger _____cm   Pinkie _____cm

Shoe width _____cm   Shoe length _____cm   Knee to floor _____cm

Circumference of neck _____cm   Chest _____cm   Waist _____cm

Weight _____kg   Weight of one shoe _____g

Length of bedroom _____m   Distance to school _____km

Many of these measurements will change. Keep your Metric Measuring License up to date. Additional copies are available in the Office.

Authenticated by Teacher: Date:

Principal's Stamp: Date:

Letter 2–22: NEW FIRST GRADE STUDENTS

TO: New First Grade Pupils
FROM: First Grade Teachers (To be read to pupils)

Welcome to first grade! I am asking your Mom or Dad to read this letter aloud to you. Now that you are ready for First Grade there are some things you should know how to do.

Before starting school you should be able to:
1. Dress yourself.
2. Tie your shoes.
3. Put on and take off your overshoes.
4. Use a handkerchief.

Do you have good health habits?
1. Do you brush your teeth?
2. Do you keep your hands clean?
3. Do you help yourself at toilet time?
4. Do you wash your hands after using the toilet?
5. Do you keep your face clean?

Please bring these things to school with you on the first day:
1. A wide–line tablet
2. Two No. 2 pencils
3. A small bottle of white glue
4. A box of crayons
5. A package of tissues

We are so glad you will be going to our school.
On the back of this paper draw a picture of your family.

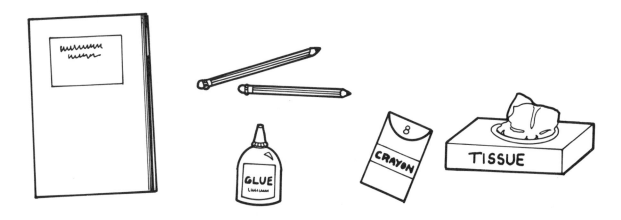

Letter 2–23: PEER TUTORING

TO: ALL STUDENTS ON THE HONOR ROLL

We are so proud of your fine record of academic success. Your outstanding schoolwork has earned you a place on our school Honor Roll. It was my pleasure to congratulate you on this accomplishment last month.

At this time I am asking you to share your skills with a less able student. We have started a Peer Tutoring service where pupils will get school help from fellow students. If you are interested, discuss this project with your parent(s) and return the brief application that appears below.

Thank you.

_____

V. DiAngelo, Principal

DETACH AND RETURN TO PRINCIPAL'S OFFICE

Dear Principal:

I am interested in serving as a Peer Tutor in this (these) subject(s):

_____   _____   _____

I can stay late 40 minutes on _____ of each week. I will be able to

begin on _____.

Pupil's Signature: _____ Date: _____

Parent's Signature: _____ Date: _____

Letter 2–24: PROGRESS

To: Charlene Paulsen   Class: 2A   Date: January 11, 19XX

Please take a moment to think about how you are doing at school. Read each statement below. Decide if you do each task always, sometimes, or never. Write in A for always, S for sometimes, or N for never, or hardly ever.

1. I follow directions. _____
2. I can work on my own. _____
3. I take care of my things. _____
4. I plan my work. _____
5. I get along with my classmates. _____
6. I am on time. _____
7. I do my homework neatly. _____
8. I like school. _____
9. I pay attention in class. _____
10. I follow school rules. _____

Now that you have finished writing in your answers, I would like to hear from you. Please write down any feelings you have about school under the word, "Comments." I promise to read your comments. If you have any suggestions about school, I would like to read them also.

Thank you,

_____

V. DiAngelo, Principal

Comments:

_____

_____

_____

Letter 2–25: PUNISHMENT

To: Harry Dibley
Class: 4C

You have been reported for the following violations of school rules:

____ Chewing gum   ____ Throwing food   ____ Running in hall
____ Cursing   ____ Hitting classmate   ____ Fighting
____ Late from lunch   ____ Destroying property   ____ Smoking

There are some very good reasons why you should not break these rules. Such behavior can be dangerous to you and to other pupils. I would like you to think about this now. Think about the good reasons for your NOT doing what you have been accused of doing.

On the back of this paper I want you to list five good reasons why you should not repeat the behavior(s) checked above. You must write five different reasons. Each reason much be written in a complete sentence.

When you have finished writing your five reasons you may write any comment you wish regarding this matter. Then, read and sign the statement below. This must be signed by your parent and returned to your teacher.

_____
V. DiAngelo, Principal

* *

Dear Principal:

I have read your statement about my breaking school rules. I have written out five reasons why I should not do this again. I (have) (have not) added a comment about how I feel about this.

_____
Pupil's Signature   Class   Date   Parent's Signature

Letter 2-26: PUPIL'S EXPLANATION FOR REFERRAL

TO: Linda Kordozian
CLASS: 5A
FROM: V. DiAngelo, Principal

You have been referred to the Office because of poor behavior/poor class work.
Please fill out this form completely and leave it on my desk. Thank you.

Name: _____ Class: _____ Date: _____

Address: _____ Phone: _____

Sent by: _____
1. Explain why you were sent to the Office:

_____

_____

2. How would you describe your behavior/work in the past?

_____

_____

3. What do you see as a possible solution to this problem?

_____

_____

_____

_____

_____

For Office Use:
      Action taken: Date:

Letter 2-27: PUPIL SAFETY RULES

To Read, Sign, and Obey

1. I will not push or touch other pupils on the class line.
2. I will not run around corners, tables, desks, or through the halls.
3. I will not accept candy, gum, treats, or rides from people I do not know well.
4. I will not throw papers, pencils, crayons, books, etc. on the classroom floor, or in the halls, or in the auditorium.
5. I will keep my lunch table and floor very clean, as if I were eating in my own house.
6. I know the best route from my house to the school. I know the basic street safety rules and follow them all the time.
7. I know the safest way to get out of my house in case of fire. I know the rules for preventing fires.
8. I have heard and follow the rules of Safety and Fire Prevention as explained to me by my teacher.
9. I will not call other pupils names, tease them, or hide their belongings.
10. I will not hit other pupils, or swing book bags, belts, or lunch boxes.
11. I will behave quietly on the bus lines and on the bus, and get on and off the bus without running or pushing.
12. I will be on my best behavior in the Auditorium during assembly programs.

    I will take this list home and go over it with my parents. After reading it I will sign it below and obey the rules.

_____

Pupil's Signature   Parent's Signature   Date

Letter 2–28: RULES

TO: Parents and Students
RE: Rules and Regulations

We want to help all our students learn in the best possible environment. To do this, the following rules and regulations have been established. Please read these rules and return the bottom portion of this sheet.

MATERIALS:

Schoolwork should be done in a loose-leaf notebook, divided into the various subjects. The student should always have two pens and two pencils. (Other materials will vary with each teacher.)

HOMEWORK:

Homework must be done each day, at home. Each student must take his or her loose-leaf notebook home every day except on Friday when there is usually no written work assigned.

FOOD:

There will be no eating of food of any kind in the classroom, and no gum chewing.

CONDUCT:

Good behavior in class means little or no talking to others; working quietly; and spending time reading or practicing skills, such as handwriting or spelling, when there is time after completing assigned work. Good conduct must also carry over into the lunchroom, schoolyard, and hallways.

DETENTION ROOM:

There will be a time set after school for students who do not follow these rules and regulations. If a student is given a Detention Notice, his or her parents will have to make the necessary transportation arrangements.

_____

V. DiAngelo, Principal

---------------------------- Please sign and return to school ----------------------------

Date _____

TO: Principal

I have read the rules and regulations and have kept the copy that was attached to this sheet.

_____ ____ _____
Student's Name   Class   Parent's Signature

Letter 2–29: RULES

RULES FOR PUPILS RIDING SCHOOL BUSES

ATTENTION: "The right of all pupils to ride on school buses is conditional on their good behavior and observance of the following rules and regulations. Any pupil who violates any of these will be reported to the school principal with the recommendation that bus privileges be suspended."
–School Board Minutes

1. The bus driver is in full charge of the bus and the pupils. Pupils shall obey the driver cheerfully and promptly.
2. Pupils shall obey and respect the orders of monitors or patrols on duty.
3. Pupils must be on time. The bus cannot wait for those who are not on time.
4. Pupils must take the seats assigned to them by the driver. They may not jump ahead of others on line.
5. Pupils may not open windows. It is absolutely forbidden for pupils to throw anything out of the bus.
6. Pupils must wait on the sidewalk or side of the road, out of the way of traffic while waiting for the bus.
7. Pupils may not change their seat once they are seated on the bus. They may not move about the bus when it is moving.
8. There will be no eating or exchanging of food on the bus.
9. Pupils who write or make any marks on the bus, windows, or seats will be suspended immediately.
10. In winter, pupils should remove as much snow as possible from their clothing before boarding the bus. Throwing snowballs at buses is absolutely forbidden.

Letter 2-30: RULES

April 3, 19XX

TO: ALL PUPILS
FR: V. DiAngelo, Principal
RE: RUNNING IN THE HALLS

By now you have heard about the accident that took place yesterday outside Room 123. One of our Third Graders was knocked down by two pupils who were running in the hall. We had to take her to the hospital where her broken arm was set in a cast.

This accident would not have taken place if all pupils followed our school rules about not running in the school building. The two boys who were running in the hall are now suspended from school. This will not help the broken arm heal faster, but I hope these boys will learn a lesson.

I hope, too, that all of you will remember not to run in the halls. If you are caught running I will make sure that you learn your lesson also.

By following this simple rule, none of you will have to worry about this serious punishment.

Letter 2-31: SCHOOL SERVICE

Dear Sixth Grader:

      In September you will be a member of the senior class and you will have a chance to serve your school community. Each year, we have seniors participating in a school service program. If you are interested, talk it over with your parents. You must have their permission before you can be accepted.
      Fill out this paper, get it signed by both your parent and teacher, and return it to my office.

      Thank you.

_____

V. DiAngelo, Principal

I would like to perform my school/community service at the following time:

_____ before school _____ after school _____ during lunch _____ on weekends

I would like to work:

_____ with young pupils _____ with classmates _____ in the office

_____ in the community _____ with the custodian _____ in the lunchroom

Teacher's Recommendation: _____

_____

_____

_____   _____

Teacher's Signature   Date

_____   _____

Parent's Signature   Date

_____   _____

Pupil's Signature   Date

Letter 2–32: SCIENCE

SCIENCE PROJECT CONTRACT   Date: _____

Pupil's Name: _____   Class: _____

Project Name: _____

1. Brief description: _____
   _____

2. Materials needed: _____
   _____

3. Library sources: _____
   _____

4. Due Date: _____

5. What form will it take: _____
   _____

6. What kind of teacher assistance will you need? _____
   _____

7. Will anyone at home help you? _____ Who? _____
   What will they do? _____
   _____

8. Which pages in our textbook will help you? _____

9. If none, list one book you will use: _____
   _____

10. Would you prefer to work with another pupil on this? _____
    Name of pupil: _____

_____   _____
Pupil's Signature   Teacher's Signature

_____
Parent's Signature

To _____

Class _____

THANK YOU FOR _____

_____

_____

_____

_____

_____

V. DiAngelo, Principal

_____

Date

Letter 2–34: SNOW

January 11, 19XX

TO: ALL PUPILS
FR: V. DiAngelo, Principal
RE: SNOWBALLS

The weatherman has announced that there will be a good chance of heavy snow tonight. If so, the school grounds will be covered with snow tomorrow. With the snow comes the temptation to throw snowballs.

Unfortunately, at school snowballs are not allowed. There are good reasons for this rule! A snowball tossed at the windshield of a school bus can cause a serious accident. A snowball thrown at a classmate could cause a bloody nose . . . or worse. In another school a "friendly snowball fight" caused a serious eye injury. A moment of careless fun could result in a lifetime of blindness.

Your Student Handbook is perfectly clear: "the throwing of snowballs is forbidden on school grounds." I'm sure you all are aware of the importance of this rule. Disciplinary action will be taken if we have any violations of this rule.

Letter 2–35: SUMMER READING LIST

TO: ALL PUPILS
RE: SUMMER READING LIST

Here are some books you may want to look for in the Library. They will help you enjoy your summer vacation.

1. Belpre, Pura. <u>Santiago</u>. Waine.
   More than anything else Santiago wants his new friend in New York to believe his stories about the beautiful pet he left behind in Puerto Rico.

2. Bemelmans, Ludwig. <u>Madeline</u>. Viking.
   Illustrations of Paris enrich the story of a little French girl and her adventures.

3. Caines, Jeannette. <u>Just Us Women</u>. Harper.
   Two women together, the young African-American narrator and her attractive and sophisticated aunt, make plans for a trip to the South on a family visit.

4. Hoban, Lillian. <u>Arthur's Funny Money</u>. Harper.
   While Arthur, an impatient monkey, faces money problems, Violet, his younger sister, struggles with math.

5. Isadora, Rachel. <u>Ben's Trumpet</u>. Greenwillow.
   Striking black and white illustrations and large, bold print portray the jazz age and a black child's yearning to play the trumpet.

6. Lobel, Arthur. <u>Takles</u>. Harper.
   Modern stories with contemporary morals written in the style of folk tales.

7. Porte, Barbara. <u>Harry's Visit</u>. Greenwillow.
   Harry finds visiting is not so bad after all.

8. Steig, William. <u>Doctor De Soto</u>. Farrar, Straus & Giroux.
   This dentist must treat large animal patients.

9. Stevenson, James. <u>We Can't Sleep</u>. Greenwillow.
   A tall tale told by a grandfather about exciting adventures.

10. Wright, Betty R. <u>My Sister is Different</u>. Raintree.
    Taking care of a retarded sister can be a nuisance, but when she gets lost in a department store, this older brother realizes how much he loves her.

Letter 2–36: SUSPENSION

Pupil Suspension Summary Form

1. Name: _____

   Address: _____

   _____

   Phone: _____

2. Date of Birth: _____ Parent's Name: _____

3. Attendance this year:

   Present _____ Absent _____ Lateness _____ Cuts _____

4. Agency, if any, to which child is known: _____

   Contact Person: _____

5. Reason for Suspension: _____

   _____

   _____

6. Date of Suspension Hearing: _____

   People present at hearing: _____

   _____

7. Has pupil been referred to Guidance: _____ Social Worker: _____

   Psychologist: _____ Behavior Counselor: _____

8. Teachers who know pupil well: _____

   _____

9. Date pupil entered school: _____

10. Previous school: _____

11. Action taken as result of hearing:

By Pupil _____

_____

_____

By School personnel _____

_____

_____

By Parent _____

_____

_____

12. Additional comments: _____

_____

_____

_____

_____

_____

_____

Letter 2–37: TESTS

TO: ALL PUPILS TAKING STANDARDIZED TESTS
RE: TECHNIQUES THAT WILL HELP YOU DO YOUR BEST

1. Before the test starts, sharpen your pencils and go to the bathroom.
2. Be sure you understand the directions before beginning to answer questions.
3. Pay attention to the time allowances for each part of the test.
4. Use your watch or the wall clock to keep track of the time. Pace yourself.
5. If you find some questions very hard, leave them and make sure you answer the questions you are sure of.
6. Use any leftover time to go back to the more difficult questions.
7. Never "give up." Use all the time allowed to go over your test and check your work.
8. Make sure the answer you fill in is for the correct question. Check from time to time that your answers match the questions.
9. Erase completely any answers you decide to change. Do not make any stray marks on your answer sheet.
10. Make sure that you have made your answers dark enough and that you have filled in the answer space completely.

Letter 2–38: UNIT OF STUDY

UNIT OF STUDY CONTRACT

I/We, the undersigned, do hereby agree to complete the following project in relation to the Unit of Study entitled: _____

_____

I/We understand the due date for completing this project is: _____

_____

In addition to the required readings, book reports, art work, audio-visuals, and oral presentation listed below, I/we will: _____

_____

_____

_____

_____

Signed on the _____ day of _____ 19____.

Student (s): _____

_____

_____

_____

_____

Teacher: _____

Letter 2–39: VANDALISM

April 18, 19XX

TO: ALL PUPILS
FR: V. DiAngelo, Principal
RE: VANDALISM

We have had several incidents of vandalism at our school recently. Windows have been broken, graffiti has been sprayed on our brick walls, and bathroom fixtures have been broken.

Sadly, whoever is responsible must have a very low opinion of himself or herself. He or she must also have a very low opinion of you, the pupils of our school. The broken windows, messy walls, and damaged bathroom fixtures place a hardship on you, the pupils.

It is going to take a lot of time and money to make the necessary repairs —money that could be better spent on computer software, athletic equipment, and art supplies.

Keep your eyes open. If you see someone vandalizing your school, let your parents or teacher know. They will decide what to do with the information. Vandalism is not a joke—it is an insult to all of us.

Letter 2–40:   YEARBOOK

Dear Boys and Girls:

This is a time for reflection and also for looking ahead. As we reflect on the past year we see that this class possessed many gifted pupils. Your reading and math scores surpassed the national and district averages. This was a spirited class that displayed many attributes of initiative and independence. (Cite one or two examples.)

You have learned many things during your years at the Spring Street School. In addition to basic knowledge and skills, you have learned how to think for yourself.

I hope that when you enter Lincoln Junior High School in the Fall you will exercise the ability to think independently. Do not fall into the trap of always following the crowd. Think for yourself and do what you think is right. Do not forget what your parents and teachers have taught you.

Good Luck!

V. DiAngelo, Principal

SECTION
3

Letters
to
Teachers

Letter 3–1: GENERAL STATEMENTS—WELCOME BACK

September 19XX

TO ALL FACULTY MEMBERS:

Welcome back! Here we are, facing another school year. The summer went quickly. I hope it was a restful time for you. If we can be certain of anything in this changing world, it is that we will be facing many challenges during this coming year as we have faced them in the past. And, as in the past, I have no doubts about your ability to meet and conquer each and every challenge.

We have dealt with challenges and obstacles with determination, tact, and the best interests of our students. Please let me know if you have any ideas about how we can achieve our goals more efficiently.

Have a very good year!

V. DiAngelo, Principal

Letter 3–2: GENERAL STATEMENTS— TEACHER HANDBOOK INTRODUCTION

Welcome to P.S. 54.

This Handbook is prepared to provide information on school policies and procedures for school personnel at P.S. 54. The Handbook is meant to supplement the School District Handbook and the School District Elementary Student Handbook with further information that directly affects the day-to-day operation of P.S. 54.

Please keep this Handbook readily available during the school year. I am sure that it will answer many questions for you. Any suggestions or recommendations for the improvement of this Handbook will be appreciated.

We are pleased to have you on our staff at P.S. 54. This Handbook will help to assist you in your teaching duties at P.S. 54. If there are any questions or concerns at any time, please feel free to see me.

_____

V. DiAngelo, Principal

Letter 3–3: GENERAL STATEMENTS—
BASIC RULES AND REGULATIONS

TO: Teachers
RE: Basic Rules and Regulations

1. No child may ever be used to render personal service for a teacher. For example, a child may not be sent to the store or to the coffee machine in the Teachers' Lounge.

2. No personal business enterprises may be conducted on school property and no unauthorized collections may be made by teachers.

3. No person may ever clock in or out for another person. Variations in time schedule are handled only by the supervisors.

4. Avoid the physical punishment of children at all times. Physical force may be used only to the extent absolutely essential for restraint in the face of danger. Corporal punishment must never be used.

5. Personnel may not leave the building during preparation periods without specific authorization from the Principal or person in charge.

6. A class may not be left uncovered and unsupervised in the course of the school day. Emergencies can be handled by contacting the office or the teacher next door.

7. Money that has been collected should not be left in the school, since the Board of Education does not take responsibility for its loss.

8. The use of the school telephone for other than school business is strictly forbidden.

9. Children should not be placed in the halls as a disciplinary measure.

10. No child may be sent home in the course of a day without office authorization. No parent may pick up a child from class without office authorization.

11. Parent-teacher conferences must not be held on class time.

12. No child is to be denied lunch without authorization.

13. No visitors should be interviewed unless they have an office pass.

14. No drug or medicine may be administered by a teacher.

15. No instructional machine or equipment may ever be removed or borrowed from school without permission and receipt from the principal. (Includes radio, recorder, phono, projector, etc.)

16. No child should be kept in school beyond 3:20 P.M. without notification to parent.

17. Personal property of pupils may not be taken without providing opportunity for retrieval by parent.

18. Funds may not be solicited from children without authorization from administrator.

19. Pupil injuries and untoward incidents must be reported to the office.

20. The teacher should lock the door when leaving the classroom.

(Please tear off and give to the principal)

I have read and understood the Basic Rules and Regulations.

Date _____   _____

                                                            Teacher's Signature

Letter 3–4: GENERAL STATEMENTS—BURNOUT

Dear Teachers,

We all need to evaluate our attitude from time to time. This checklist will help you reduce your burnout factor.

DO YOU KNOW . . .

1. That besides mother and father, you are the most important person in the world to most children?
2. That many children want to be just like you?
3. That the funny-nosed boy in the third row might become the doctor who saves your life?
4. That the scientists working to protect your future once sat in a classroom at the grade level which you teach?
5. That lifelong scars are caused by a single statement made by teachers?
6. That almost every "off-the-cuff" remark that you make is retold over the supper table?
7. That children respect a tough teacher more than a pushover?

DO YOU . . .

1. Ever hate Monday?
2. Ever call a child "dumb"?
3. Really like children?
4. Ever transfer that feeling to your students?
5. Ever pay as much attention to the girl with ragged shoes as to the one with new patent leather shoes.
6. Ever come to school unprepared?
7. Ever get angry when your students do the same?
8. Ever rebel at that "extra" that's asked of you?
9. Really like teaching?

WILL YOU . . .

1. Take a sincere interest in every student who enters your classroom?
2. Stand by and support your fellow teachers in all of their school endeavors?
3. Support your P.T.A.?
4. Strengthen yourself by taking college courses?
5. Continue to read and bring yourself up to date in the field of education?

Letter 3–5: GENERAL STATEMENTS— CLASSROOM ASSISTANTS

TO: Early Childhood Teachers
FR: V. DiAngelo, Principal
RE: Using Classroom Assistants

Many Early Childhood classes will be fortunate to have a paraprofessional, parent or community volunteer assistant and/or student teacher. These adults can support the teaching/learning process in providing for:

- additional small group activities, such as making play dough, playing a lotto game, telling a story
- individual attention, observing a child's behavior patterns
- preparation of materials
- group activities outside of the classroom, such as, a trip within the school, picking up lunch or snack in the lunchroom, borrowing books from the school library

When classroom assistants are available on a regular basis, the teacher should:

- welcome their support.
- meet regularly to establish consistent routines, share information, plan together.
- assign specific tasks or areas of concentration, such as: responsibility for classroom library (helping children select a story, selecting books about a theme for display, reading a story).
- discuss aspects of child development; for example, children grow at different rates and have different learning styles.
- ask about their special interests. (Some of the assistants may play a musical instrument or have skills in working with wood or other raw materials.)
- encourage assistants to sit at eye level with children, listening to and joining these activities when appropriate. For example, in the housekeeping area, other adults can extend children's language and dramatic play by asking questions, such as, "What does the family do after breakfast?"
- ask assistants to help in transition by encouraging children to clean up after finishing tasks, (e.g. putting away collage materials, rewinding tape recorder).
- encourage assistants to maintain their role as adults in the classroom.
- provide time to share skills. The teacher may model techniques in working with a flannel board. The volunteer, paraprofessional or student teacher may know how to care for a pet animal, or sing songs in another language.

Every classroom is enriched by a classroom assistant. Children gain by interacting with other children and with adults who are knowledgeable and caring. It is important that these additional supportive adults allow children to work, play, and "do it themselves" in this critical year of growing and learning.

Letter 3–6: GENERAL STATEMENTS— LAST DAY PROCEDURES

TO: P.S. 54 Staff   June 1, 19XX

RE: Procedures for the last day of school

Please check your copy of the Teacher's Handbook, issued to you in September, for detailed instructions concerning each of the following items. All of these items must be checked and turned in before you will receive your June paycheck.

1. Makeup tests to be administered where needed or a statement signed by you that none of your students are eligible for summer make-up testing.

2. Your grade book with all marks complete. This will be reviewed by your head of department.

3. Your roll book with complete attendance summary (for homeroom teachers only).

4. All keys (desk, room, closet). Place keys in an envelope with your name and room number on it. Any keys missing must be noted on the face of the envelope.

5. Your Library Clearance Form indicating that all books have been returned.

On the last day of school, June 24, a table will be set up in the Faculty Cafeteria and staffed by our two assistant principals. Turn in the materials called for above. Each item will be checked by an assistant principal and initialed. Take this checked form to the General Office and one of the school secretaries will give you your check.

Please accept my best wishes for a happy and healthful summer vacation.

V. DiAngelo

_____   _____
Teacher's Name   Assistant Principal's Signature

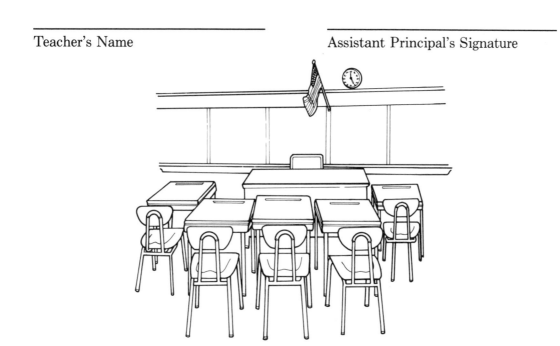

Letter 3-7: GENERAL STATEMENTS—NEW PROGRAM

TO: Faculty
RE: New Program

    No new program comes to us error-proof and problem-free. The new program that goes into effect next week will be no exception. I know, however, that there is no problem that we cannot solve if we work together, as we have so many times in the past.

    You are a credit to our profession. As educators, we realize that education is an ongoing process. It is something developmental that tries to evaluate but sometimes fails. However, we strive for the best of which we are capable. I have seen you work on this new program and give your time and efforts to give it the chance it deserves. I am proud of that fact, and no one could ask for more.

    As this new program begins, I want you to know that I support and applaud your efforts. Working together, there is nothing we cannot accomplish.

V. DiAngelo, Principal

Letter 3–8: GENERAL STATEMENTS—OPEN HOUSE

TO: Faculty
FROM: V. DiAngelo, Principal
RE: Reflections on the "Open House"

As you know, several days ago we held our annual Open House for the community. It was a huge success. I have been deluged with phone calls from parents and community members telling me how impressed they were with what they saw and praising you, the faculty, for the fine job you are doing. I want to express to you my appreciation for a job well done.

I am grateful for the support, the cooperation, and the dedication that has made my job easier and made our school the fine place it is for all of the children.

Thank you.

Letter 3-9: GENERAL STATEMENTS—POLICY

TO: All Teachers
RE: Policy Statement on Pupil Notebooks

Pupils should seldom leave a class without having noted some important ideas of that period's lesson in their notebooks. Generally, notebook recording should take place at the end of the lesson in the form of summary notes or a homework assignment, but recording often takes place at the beginning of a lesson in response to review questions, homework reviewing, or orientation for the day's lesson.

1. Notebook recording is valuable because it:
   - Provides a change of activity from discussion, demonstration, drill, etc.
   - Gives the teacher a chance for pupil individualization while the class is busy.
   - Provides the teacher with both a subjective and objective evaluation procedure for pupil rating.
   - Gives both teacher and pupil "capsule" ideas for a lesson—for review and tests.
   - Often clarifies thinking for teacher and pupils.
   - Provides pupils with practice in summary note taking and writing.
   - Shows parents what the pupil has learned in class.
   - Provides practice in handwriting.

2. In order to motivate pupils to bring notebooks and pens or pencils to every class, teachers should:
   - Have interesting, important information on the chalkboard for each period and insist that pupils record it in their notebooks.
   - Regularly check and mark pupils' notebooks to ensure continued motivation.
   - Keep a record of pupils who neglect to bring notebooks or writing implements; but provide them with paper or pencil to record notebook work.
   - Warn pupils who chronically fail to bring notebooks or refuse to do notebook work in class of the consequences.

_____

V. DiAngelo, Principal

Letter 3-10: GENERAL STATEMENTS—PUBLICITY

TO: All Teachers
FR: V. DiAngelo, Principal

   I am seeking information about students in our schools who have made an important contribution or achieved a noteworthy distinction, especially in the area of academic achievement.
   If you have a student who fits this description, please complete this page and return it to me. (Teachers or other school employees might also qualify if they have contributed "above and beyond" the call of duty in furthering academic achievement.)
   We will use the information you provide to promote community recognition of our outstanding students. Examples of the type of student(s) we are looking for include:

1. a student who has won an academic award
2. a student who has a straight "A" record for several successive years
3. a student who has overcome his or her handicaps to achieve a significant honor
4. a student who has completed a major achievement, such as winning a district-wide contest or completing an outstanding science project
5. a student or group of students who have made an important contribution to the school (or community)
6. a student with unusual artistic abilities, such as art or music
7. a student who has won a special citation from a local agency or organization

Name of Individual: _____ Class: _____

Address: _____ Age: _____

Brief Description: _____

_____

_____

_____

_____

Letter 3–11: GENERAL STATEMENTS—
SCHOOL TELEPHONE

TO: All Staff Members
FR: V. DiAngelo, Principal
RE: Use of the School Telephone

Our school telephone bill is monitored by the District Office. In recent months several toll calls have appeared on our bill that I cannot explain. This has become a source of great embarrassment and needless expense to me and our school.

You are reminded that the expense of all toll calls for personal reasons must be borne by the staff member making the call. Also, be sure to record all official toll calls in the telephone log on my secretary's desk before making such calls. In this way we can anticipate the long distance charges before they appear.

The pay phone outside Room 101 is available to you for personal calls. You may charge calls to your home phone on the pay phone.

Your cooperation is appreciated.

Letter 3–12: GENERAL STATEMENTS—TRIPS

TO: Classroom Teachers
FR: V. DiAngelo, Principal
RE: Rules for Trips

1. Pupils and teachers should plan the trip together. Included in the planning should be:

   a. Purpose of the trip (what do we want to find out?).
   b. Details of transportation (time, costs, etc.)
   c. Briefing of pupils on their responsibilities as representatives of the school (including behavior and attire).
   d. Briefing of pupils on what they will see and do.
   e. Provision for evaluation and follow-up.

   Pupils must understand that the purpose of the trip is primarily educational and not recreational. They must understand that the learning experiences of the trip will be discussed and evaluated later and that the trip is part of their curriculum just as much as the textbook work or classroom discussion.

   Do not take trips to places that your pupils have already visited.

2. Procedures for Arranging Trips

   Teachers planning to take a trip should first secure the approval of the principal. The District Office will not approve trips to movie theaters.

   After obtaining the necessary approval, the teacher will arrange for the trip with the agency or place to be visited. Following the confirmation of the date scheduled, the attached form must be filled out. Be accurate! List each class and the number of pupils. All pupils in the class should be taken!

   Arrangements must be completed and approval from District Office obtained at least two weeks before the trip. DO NOT telephone the District Office—all arrangements will be made in writing.

3. A Few Do's and Don'ts

   a. Do your best to adhere to your time schedule while on your trip. Call the school in case you are delayed or if a problem arises.
   b. Instruct pupils taking the trip not to arrive at school too early. Teachers conducting the trip must arrive at school early enough to supervise the arrival of pupils.
   c. Speak to your supervisor before the trip to obtain information as to where the pupils may wait for the arrival of the chartered bus. Proper planning will prevent confusion.
   d. Trips are made from the school; we are responsible for the pupils until they return to school! DO NOT allow pupils to leave the bus in order that they may have a shorter trip home.
   e. Before leaving the school the teacher must have a consent slip for each pupil and a passenger manifest listing the pupils who actually went on the trip. No pupil may accompany a teacher on a trip unless a parental consent slip is on file.
   f. If you have any difficulty with the bus company, let your supervisor know.

Letter 3–13: CURRICULUM—ASSEMBLIES

TO: All Teachers
FR: V. DiAngelo, Principal
RE: Criteria for Assembly Programs

Each class shall be responsible for putting on one assembly program.

This will be a pupil activity in the form of a play, choral speaking, dance program, or singing of seasonal songs.

It should be a pupil-centered activity as opposed to a film or guest speaker. You may find it helpful to use this ten-point list of pupil criteria.

1. When should the program be given?
2. What format should be used for the program?
3. Which plays are suitable for this audience?
4. Who should be the announcer?
5. What will he be expected to do?
6. Who is to be invited?
7. Who should design the invitations?
8. What four things should be included in the invitation? (date, time, place, event)
9. Which children will make up a committee to greet the guest?
10. Who will set up the program?

Letter 3–14: CURRICULUM—BOOK REPORTS

TO: Teachers
FR: V. DiAngelo, Principal
RE: Alternates to Standard Book Report

Children and parents tire of the standard book report. The pupil reads a book, enjoys the experience and then faces the drudgery of writing a standard book report. Here are a dozen suggestions that provide enjoyable, painless alternatives.

1. Write a letter recommending the book to a friend.
2. Pretend you are a newspaper reporter writing a review of the book for the newspaper.
3. Make an attractive book jacket; summarize the story on the "flaps."
4. Construct a crossword puzzle about people and events in the story.
5. Write a letter to the author and discuss the book.
6. Create a story of your own with the same title. How does it differ from the one you read?
7. Read an especially exciting chapter aloud to a friend. See if he or she can accurately predict the outcome of the book.
8. Make paper puppets and prepare a show about the book.
9. Design a simple "roller movie" on shelf paper showing major events in the book. Use captions or "conversation bubbles."
10. Dress as a character or object in the book and tell the story from his, her, or its point of view.
11. Make a shoe-box diorama of a favorite scene. Write an explanatory description for interested viewers.
12. Create your own project to be discussed with the teacher.

Letter 3–15: CURRICULUM—CLASS PAPERS

TO: Teachers
FR: V. DiAngelo, Principal
RE: Class Papers Cover Letter

Teacher _____ Class _____ Date _____

Aim of this set of papers:

Motivation/Instruction in creative expression:

Strengths noted:

      Class

      Individual

Weaknesses noted:

      Class

      Individual

Follow-up lessons:

Teacher's Assessment of these papers:

Names of pupils with very good and very poor papers:

Names of pupils showing much improvement:

Letter 3–16: CURRICULUM—DEATH

TO: Teacher
FR: V. DiAngelo, Principal
RE: Helping Students Cope with Death

The subject of death may come up in classroom discussions. Children hear and see a lot about dying and are curious. They have questions. There are also situations that arise in which the classroom teacher may be called upon to help students cope with the effects of death. This fact sheet has been designed to help you. The following information may be helpful in working with and understanding student reactions.

1. Children's perceptions of death will vary with their developmental stage, individual life experiences, and family influences. No two children will react to death in exactly the same way. Some children have experienced the death of a pet or grandparent. Others have never experienced a loss. Some children come from families that talk very openly about death. Other families choose not to discuss the subject. These experiences will all affect how a student reacts to death.

2. Before ages 5 or 6, the child sees death as something temporary. There is no definitive death. The dead person will return and resume his other normal activities. Children at this age also have considerable faith in their own ability to make things happen, simply by wishing.

3. As they grow toward age 6, children begin to see death as permanent. During this developmental stage, children may become increasingly anxious about death. They often associate death with violence. Death is final, but it is not natural and not inevitable. It is not something that happens to them.

4. The third stage begins at about age 9. Death is seen as final and inevitable. Children from 10 to 12 years of age are ready to deal with the reality of death but find the idea that death can happen to anyone at any age difficult to accept. Ten-to-twelve-year-olds may cover their fears about death by joking about and making fun of death. This is an attempt to protect themselves from something they do not completely understand.

5. Making fun of and joking about death carries over into adolescence. Adolescence adds another facet to coping with death. Children at this age tend to defy the inevitability of death—a kind of "I dare it to happen to me" attitude. Their behavior exhibits a need to prove they are immune.

6. Children who experience a loss will generally exhibit shock, numbness, and denial. They may then experience anger toward the deceased. "Daddy didn't love me. He had no right to leave me like this." This may be followed by anger toward the survivor. These reactions are often followed by guilt. The child may feel some responsibility for the death. "If I'd been good . . ." They may also experience a fear of losing someone else or of dying themselves. Children, like adults, go through a grief process. It is important that they know it is okay to cry or express other emotions. It is important, too, that they have someone they can talk to about what has happened. Do not hesitate to refer a pupil to our guidance counselor or a school administrator if you have any serious concern about his/her reactions.

Letter 3–17: CURRICULUM—KINDERGARTEN

KINDERGARTEN NEEDS ASSESSMENT

Last Name	First Name	Sex

Indicate the child's ability to complete the tasks asked. Use the ratings of: C = Comfortably, D = with Difficulty, N = Not at all.

1. States his or her whole name. _____

2. States his or her address. _____

3. States his or her telephone number. _____

4. Prints his or her own name from memory. _____

5. Places pictures in sequential order. _____

6. Distinguishes left hand from right hand. _____

7. Expresses ideas in complete sentences. _____

8. Repeats four digits in forward order. _____

9. Identifies numerals. _____

10. Identifies coins. _____

11. Recognizes size ____ shape ____ color ____ of objects. _____

12. Adds and subtracts in problem situations. _____

13. Copies simple shapes. _____

14. Erects a balanced structure. _____

15. Sits still for a reasonable time. _____

16. Appears in Good ____ Fair ____ Poor ____ health. _____

17. Provides uses for a common object. e.g., string. (number stated) _____

18. Draws a picture of a person. (number of details/ completeness) _____

19. Speaks English. _____

COMMENTS: _____

_____

_____

Letter 3–18: CURRICULUM—MAINSTREAMING

TO: Regular and Special Education Teachers

In order to accommodate our Special Education children in "mainstream" activities please examine this checklist.

1. Strategies for mainstreaming include:
   - lunchroom/recess/lineup
   - assembly programs
   - special school events
   - combined gym schedules
   - peer-tutoring programs
   - big brother programs
   - assignment of individual children to regular classes for specific periods of time
   - club programs
   - monitor service
   - special school programs; e.g., chorus, band

2. Some tasks and suggestions for developing and mainstreaming program include:
   - develop positive attitudes and acceptance
   - involve parents of mainstreamed child
   - develop pupil awareness and acceptance
   - use buddy system in the classroom
   - move slowly and plan carefully
   - provide time for special education teacher/regular classroom teacher to discuss child's needs, curriculum adaptation.
   - provide assistance where necessary to help children move about the building.
   - inform and instruct the school's regular P.A./P.T.A. regarding process and enlist their help.
   - consult with special education supervisor, guidance counselor, other appropriate personnel.
   - evaluate progress for possible return to a less restrictive environment.

Letter 3-19: CURRICULUM—READING

TO: Teachers
RE: Reading Interest Inventory

Before you can plan enjoyable, meaningful activities for your pupils, you need to know what your students' interests are. This Reading Interest Inventory will help you.

1. In my free time I like to . . .
2. I like people who . . .
3. I like to read books about . . .
4. My favorite author is . . .
5. When I grow up I want to be . . .
6. I don't like books that . . .
7. I'd like to go . . .
8. My favorite time to read is . . .
9. The thing I like to read most is . . .
10. I like to read aloud to . . .
11. What I want most in the world is . . .
12. I like books with . . .
13. I wish . . .
14. Reading makes me . . .

Letter 3–20: CURRICULUM—READING

TO: Teachers on Grade
RE: Selecting a Reading Series

    We want your input in selecting a new reading series for your grade. Since you are the classroom teacher who will use the new readers, I value your opinion. Please use a scale of 1 to 5 for each item (5 being excellent and 1 being poor).

Name of Series: _____

Publisher: _____

Copyright date: _____

    1. Readability: (vocabulary; sentence and paragraph length) ____

    2. Content: (balance of real and imaginery; poetry; etc.) ____

    3. Teaching process: (decoding instruction; vocabulary strands; comprehension) ____

    4. Evaluation: (placement tests; inventories; posttesting) ____

    5. Teacher's edition: ____

    6. Workbook: ____

    7. Other Teacher Aids: ____

    8. Physical features: (visuals; durability; format) ____

COMMENTS _____

_____

_____

_____
Teacher's Name

_____   _____
Class   Date

Letter 3–21: CURRICULUM—TESTS

TO: Teachers
RE: Staff Preparation for Testing

Even when you have prepared students to be better test takers and are working to involve parents in their child's education, your task is still not complete! You, too, need to prepare yourself to give tests. The following is a list of things for staff to do to "be prepared." (If students only knew!)

1. Preparing yourself

   - Review the test and the administration manual. Be especially familiar with the directions for students.
   - Make sure you have enough test booklets, answer sheets, scratch paper, and pencils.
   - Know which students are to be tested.
   - Decide what you will do with students who come late (a tardy room with an alternative testing schedule?) and with students who finish the test early (perhaps provide books, magazines, newspapers, or appropriate assignments).
   - Know the dates of testing and makeup testing.
   - Be positive about the testing.

2. Preparing the place

   - Provide students with comfortable seats with smooth, hard, writing surfaces large enough for a folded test booklet and an answer sheet.
   - Seat students so that they are not able to see the answers of others.
   - Make sure you will be heard clearly by all students.
   - Decide if you need proctors to assist you and the students.
   - Test in a room that has good lighting, adequate ventilation, and is free of noise and interruptions.
   - Arrange for rooms well before the test is to be given. Students' regular classrooms should be first choice.
   - Test in classroom-size groups, when possible.

3. Physical readiness

In addition to knowing something about the test itself, students need to know how to prepare physically and emotionally to take the test. The two most important physical preparations to discuss with students involve sleep and food.

- The night before the test, students should have at least eight hours of sleep.
- The day of the test, students should have proper nourishment: breakfast is a must before a morning test as is lunch before an afternoon test.
- Students should wear something comfortable but also appropriate for the temperature of the room where testing will be done.

4. Emotional readiness

On the emotional level, a student's performance on the test is often adversely affected by lack of self-confidence, lack of motivation, and text anxiety. Frequent, positive statements by teachers during regular class sessions can enhance students' overall self-confidence. At test time, encouragement to students and positive statements about their abilities by the test giver can promote feelings of self-confidence.

Motivating students, or helping them to motivate themselves, is also important. Help students get in the right frame of mind by:

- Removing the threat aspect of testing;
- emphasizing that the test is a chance for them to show how much they know, to show how good they are; and,
- reminding them that they must try hard in order to do the job well.

Letter 3-22: CURRICULUM—TESTS

TO: Teachers
FR: V. DiAngelo, Principal
RE: Procedures for Administering Standardized Test

1. Before the test:
   - After clocking in on Tuesday morning, pick up from Mrs. Santoro in the office:

     1 package of tests and answer sheets
     1 box of pencils
     1 stopwatch
   - Place on outside of classroom door a sign reading, "Testing today, do not enter."

2. During the test:
   - Keep a record of the time for the test on the chalkboard.
   - Do not allow children to leave the room after the test has begun.
   - Be an active proctor. Walk around the room but do not disturb the pupils.

3. After the test:
   - Collect booklets and check them for completeness, including the identifying data on the cover sheet.
   - Write names of absentees on the outside of the brown envelope.
   - Alphabetize the answer sheets—boys and girls separately.
   - Return test, pencils, and stopwatch—personally—to Mrs. Santoro.
   - Arrangements will be made by the office to test absentees.

Letter 3–23: LESSON PLANS— INDIVIDUAL LESSON PLAN

INDIVIDUAL LESSON PLAN

CLASS _____ DATE _____

UNIT _____ TOPIC _____

BEHAVIORAL OBJECTIVE(S) _____

_____

_____

_____

TIME ALLOTMENT   ACTIVITIES

ASSIGNMENT

_____

_____

_____

MATERIALS   REFERENCES

_____   _____

_____   _____

_____   _____

_____   _____

Letter 3–24: LESSON PLANS—PLAN BOOK

TO: Teachers
FR: V. DiAngelo, Principal
RE: Plan Book Suggestions

Please review your Plan Book. Check to see how well it meets these guidelines:

1. Your Plan Book
    a. Helps to organize, systemize, and record teaching.
    b. Guides the substitute teacher.
    c. Helps to develop skills sequentially.
    d. Indicates to supervisors the progress of the program.
    e. Gives supervisor a key to the kind of help a teacher needs.
    f. Helps teacher to evaluate pupil's needs and learning.

2. It Should:
    a. Adapt the curriculum to special needs of pupils.
    b. Provide stimulating materials that are conducive to pupil growth.
    c. Include all curriculum areas designated by the particular school.
    d. Provide sequence in subject matter and continuity of learnings in the designated curriculum areas.
    e. Unify knowledge by integrating curriculum areas in the interest of economy of time.
    f. Use all available resources.
    g. Indicate experiences for class, groups, and individuals.
    h. Provide for maximum pupil participation in class and school activities.
    i. Continue evaluation and follow-up of class, group and individual progress.
    j. Record work completed and of changes needed.
    k. Include daily skills; lessons in areas of need such as in reading, handwriting, and in mathematics.
    l. Indicate lesson aim, procedure, textbook pages, class activity assignment, and homework in major subject areas.
    m. Indicate individual help to be provided.

Letter 3–25: LESSON PLANS—PLAN BOOK

COMMENTS ON PLAN BOOK

_____   _____

Teacher's Name   Class

A review of your lesson plan reveals the following:

Items Missing   General Comments

_____ content area (   )   _____ plans are incomplete

_____ related material   _____ plans are vague

_____ pupil assignment   _____ plans are late

_____ remedial material   _____ plans are not appropriate

_____ enrichment material   _____ plans are satisfactory

_____ object of lesson   _____ plans are outstanding

Additional Comments: _____

_____

_____

_____

Signature of Principal: _____ Date: _____

Signature of Teacher: _____ Date: _____

Letter 3–26: LESSON PLANS—PLANNING CHECKLIST

TO: Early Childhood Teachers
RE: Planning Checklist for the Early Childhood Teacher

- Make certain that the children will have a relaxed, unhurried school day with easy transitions from one activity to another.
- Plan so that children have the opportunities to make choices and decisions.
- Include the assistant and cluster personnel in planning and confer with them regarding the plan.
- Develop activities around a current interest or theme.
- Build on the experiences of previous days.
- Evaluate carefully the experiences and materials to be used and select those that will afford optimum development.
- Alternate the scheduling of active and quiet activities.
- Maintain a balance of individual, group, and entire class activities.
- Provide an opportunity to rest during both the morning and afternoon sessions.
- Include time each day for planning and evaluating the day's work.
- Schedule a snack at midsession.
- Provide an opportunity for some outdoor play every day, weather permitting.
- Include frequent, well-planned trips in the school and around the community.

Letter 3–27: CLASSROOM—APPEARANCE

January 22, 19XX
CLASS: 3A

Dear Ms. Buckner,

We have met several times for the purpose of improving the appearance of your classroom. Beginning on December 13, mutual plans were established for specific ways in which you could better organize and maintain your classroom both to improve its general appearance and effectiveness as a learning environment. We met twice again on January 7 and January 14, following planned visits to review the improvements.

Despite these meetings, plans, and visits, I find no improvement in either the appearance or organization of your classroom. The students in your class are learning habits of disorder both for their own learning process as well as for school property.

This situation cannot continue. Your classroom must show a marked improvement as outlined in our discussion or I will be forced to take further action. If you no longer have a copy of the notes of our meeting, an additional copy may be obtained from the secretary.

I sincerely hope that you will be able to take the necessary actions to make your room acceptable so that further action on my part will not be necessary.

Sincerely,

_____

V. DiAngelo, Principal

I have read this letter and understand
that it will be placed in my file.

_____

Teacher's Signature

cc: Teacher

Letter 3–28: CLASSROOM—BULLETIN BOARDS

TO: All Teachers
RE: Bulletin Boards

Your classroom and hall bulletin boards are basically the "windows" of the room, the teacher, the pupils, and the school. Visitors note bulletin boards first. However, more important than what visitors note is the fact that the effectiveness of teaching is usually revealed in the appearance and content of the bulletin boards.

Some Hints for Effective Bulletin Boards

1. Change displays frequently. Plan displays with pupils.

2. Displays should indicate the subject and include captions.

3. Make bulletin boards "conversation pieces"—colorful, inviting, creative, and informative.

4. Consult other members of the faculty for ideas—color, contrast, creative background.

5. Paper used for mounting pictures should follow a consistent color scheme, chosen to harmonize with the bulletin board's color.

6. If two or more units or topics are on display, they should be mounted, arranged, and titled distinctively with sufficient intervening space to avoid a run-together appearance.

7. Small headings may be lettered in a single stroke manuscript style. Large headings should be in block letters. Pre-stamped letters are good for this.

8. Use staples where possible. Tacks are a possible hazard and cellulose tape is not as neat looking.

9. Use guide lines for lettering so that the lettering is neat.

10. Have good balance. DO NOT CLUTTER. ALLOW FOR HIGHLIGHTS.

11. There are many things that can be displayed:

    – booklets made by the pupils

    – good work of children

    – illustrated book reports

    – current events—with pupil captions

    – relevant pictures (with captions)

    – graphs

    – illustrations drawn by pupils

Letter 3-29: CLASSROOM—CLEANLINESS

TO: All Teachers
RE: General Rules for Classroom Cleanliness

Each teacher is responsible for the care and cleanliness of the room as it pertains to book storage, shelves, teacher's desk, etc.

You are asked to make provision or provide procedures to take care of the following:

1. Students should pick up all paper, pencils, etc., from the floor around their desks at the end of the school day.

2. Students should remove everything from the tops of their desks at the end of the school day. Books and personal items should be picked up from the floor at the end of the day.

3. Check on keeping shelves, tables, desks, etc., in an orderly manner at the end of each school day. Your desk should be tidied up before leaving school for the night.

4. Close all windows when leaving the room at the end of the school day.

5. Please use discretion on taping things to the walls or chalkboards in the classrooms. Items taped to the walls or windows with masking tape should not be left too long as the glue will separate from the tape and deface the wall, boards, etc., after a period of time. Tape can ruin chalkboards by taking off coating finish.

6. Be sure that outside doors lock behind you when you leave the building. (The doors close, but often do not lock. Please check them.)

7. Students should be encouraged to respect the building as part of their civic responsibility and respect for public property. Please note the following:

   a. There is absolutely no need for writing on or defacing any part of the building, equipment, or grounds. Violations will be dealt with through the principal's office.

   b. Students should clean off their shoes and boots before coming into the building in wet and muddy weather.

   c. No writing or marking on desks or walls.

8. Rooms with carpet: Exercise good judgment and care in the use of glue and clay; it is very hard to get that out of the carpet.

Letter 3–30: CLASSROOM—ENVIRONMENT

TO: Classroom Teacher
RE: Your Classroom Environment

PART I—The Room's Appearance

_____ 1. Does the appearance of the room reflect a sense of functional arrangement and orderliness?

_____ 2. Is the room aesthetically pleasing?

_____ 3. Is the room interesting and inviting?

_____ 4. Is the room well ventilated?

_____ 5. Is the room divided into clearly defined centers of interest?

_____ 6. Is there a quiet area children may use?

_____ 7. Is furniture arranged to fit children's needs?

_____ 8. Are there open lanes to travel from center to center?

_____ 9. Can the furniture be moved easily to meet the needs of an activity? (snack time, rhythms)

_____ 10. Is there an area of the room for group meetings or large group instruction?

_____ 11. Are tables arranged in groups?

_____ 12. Is the piano placed so that the teacher can see all of the children at one time?

_____ 13. Does each child have an individual storage space? Is the block area adequate in size and in a safe place away from interruptions?

_____ 14. Is there a place to put completed work?

_____ 15. Are bulletin boards current, functional, and at children's eye level?

_____ 16. Is there access to a water source, and a child-sized restroom facilities?

_____ 17. Is there a place for drying paintings?

_____ 18. Is there a writing area stocked with paper, pencils, dictionaries, typewriter?

PART II—Materials of Instruction

_____ 1. Do children know where the materials are kept?

_____ 2. Is there adequate storage for all materials?

_____ 3. Is there convenient access to materials?

_____ 4. Is equipment kept clean and are broken items discarded?

_____ 5. Do the children know the uses of each object in the area?

_____ 6. Are directions posted?

_____ 7. Are there materials available for creative activities such as boxes, buttons, scrap material, wood, etc.?

_____ 8. Are reference materials available to extend learning developed in a particular area?

_____ 9. Does the room have live plants and pets?

_____ 10. Is there a variety of types of books, tapes, records, filmstrips?

_____ 11. Are materials and visual aids changed often to maintain interest?

_____ 12. Are materials provided for individualized work?

_____ 13. Is there a variety of hands-on experiences available?

_____ 14. Are there cleanup materials such as sponges, paper towels?

_____ 15. Is there a place for everything?

_____ 16. Are there materials for dramatic play such as shoes, pocketbooks, empty food boxes, etc.?

_____ 17. Is there a variety of basic visual art media?

_____ 18. Are there small manipulative materials to build eye-hand coordination?

_____ 19. Are field trips included as learning experiences?

_____ 20. Are there seasonal interests for children to observe?

_____ 21. Are there cooking experiences?

_____ 22. Are there materials for music and rhythmic experiences?

Part III—Children and Program

_____ 1. Are the children aware of their responsibility for the appearance of the room?

_____ 2. Are children's experiences used as a basis for oral discussion?

_____ 3. Are sensory experiences used as a basis for oral discussion?

_____ 4. Is children's work attractively displayed and current?

_____ 5. Is a name tag fastened to the picture?

_____ 6. Are pictures changed frequently?

_____ 7. Are children encouraged to care for live plants and pets in the room?

_____ 8. Are there opportunities for reading around the room? Are pictures/charts attractive and at the eye level of the child? Is the writing on charts and labels clear and legible?

_____ 9. Are there opportunities for language development?

_____ 10. Are there opportunities for the children to make specific choices?

_____ 11. Are children encouraged to share materials?

_____ 12. Do children have opportunities for writing experiences?

_____ 13. Does the program balance individual, group, and full class activities?

_____ 14. Is there integration of curriculum areas?

Letter 3–31: CLASSROOM—RECESS CLEANUP

TO: Teachers
RE: Winter Recess Room Cleanup

During the winter recess your room will be cleaned by the custodial staff. Please help by seeing to it that the following items are taken care of.

1. Begin to dispose of unwanted papers and materials today. Do not wait until the day before the holiday.
2. Clear off all cabinet tops.
3. Store all materials in closets. Remove jars of paint and put easels in wardrobes.
4. Leave nothing (brief cases, book bags, sneakers, etc.) on the floor of the room or coat closet.
5. Have pupils empty their desks. Pupils' books may be stored in closets or taken home on a staggered basis.
6. Clear off window sills. Send plants home.
7. Remove decorations from doors and windows.
8. Clean out chalk troughs. Have pupils wash boards.
9. Be sure that children take home pets and fish.
10. If you are having a class party do NOT have it on the last day of school. Have it on the day before instead.

HAVE A HAPPY AND ENJOYABLE HOLIDAY!

Letter 3–32: OBSERVATION OF LESSONS—CHECKLIST

November 5, 19XX

TO: Mrs. Hoogerhyde
CLASS: 2A

I plan to observe you teach a lesson on November 10 in the area of science. These are the criteria I plan to use. Please refer to this list in planning your lesson.

1. State objective or aim.
2. Objectively state lesson development and activities.
3. List materials used.
4. Record follow-up activities.
5. Describe evaluation methods.
6. Include comments (in the order and degree of importance in this situation) that discuss:
   a. appropriateness of lesson
      • to class   • to curriculum
   b. development of lesson
      • motivation   • medial summary   • final summary
      • sequential development
   c. individualization
      • provision for differences   • adaptation of material
   d. classroom environment
      • special interest or learning centers   • use of chalkboard
      • furniture arrangement   • cleanliness/attractiveness
      • evidence of pupil work
   e. questioning techniques (see Board of Education publication on Questioning)
   f. relationships
      • teacher-pupil   • pupil-pupil
   g. routines of behavior management
   h. activities
      • variety   • multisensory approaches
   i. ability to perceive and adjust to immediate needs
   j. teacher manner
7. Recommended improvements as discussed in post observation conference.
8. Indicate whether lesson was satisfactory or unsatisfactory.

V. DiAngelo, Principal

Letter 3–33: OBSERVATION OF LESSONS— EVALUATION

TO: Teachers Being Observed
RE: Suggestions for Evaluating Your Lesson

1. What was the aim of your lesson? To what extent is it worthy? Definite? Specific with regard to this class? Attainable?

2. To what extent did the students share in proposing the aim? To what extent do they comprehend and adopt the aim proposed by the teacher?

3. What was the appropriateness of the type of recitation and/or activity used to achieve the aim?

4. How suitable was the plan for achieving the desired objectives?

5. Was your preparation adequate? How is preparation or lack of preparation evidenced in the lesson?

6. What assignment has been made? To what extent does it conform to the criteria for good assignments? How effective is it when judged by the responses of the students?

7. How were pupils' preparation and past learnings or experiences used in the lesson?

8. How did the students behave, as shown by good manners and respect?

9. What concomitant learnings did you encourage and direct?

10. How suitable were the materials used in the lesson? How well were they managed and used?

11. To what extent was the aim of the lesson carried through and achieved?

12. What were the outcomes in terms of knowledge, concepts, skills, attitudes? What evidence was there that the lesson was learned?

13. What provisions were made for summaries or "fixing the learnings"?

14. What provisions were made for individual differences in interest, needs, special aptitudes, and ability?

15. How much participation in the recitation was there by the students? In planning? In active contributions? In activities? In evaluation?

Letter 3–34: OBSERVATION OF LESSONS— INTERVISITATION

TO: Buddy Teacher
RE: Record of Intervisitation Form

1. Name of Teacher-Observer _____ Class_____

2. Teacher-Demonstrator _____ Class_____

3. Subject of Lesson _____
4. Brief Description:

5. Date of Intervisitation _____
6. Time of Visit:

    Began at: _____ A.M./P.M.   Ended at: _____ A.M./P.M.
7. Signatures of:

_____   _____

Teacher-Demonstrator   Teacher-Observer

Letter 3–35: OBSERVATION OF LESSONS— OBSERVATION

April 30, 19XX
CLASS: 3B

Dear Mr. Zimmerman:

I am planning to observe you teach a lesson of approximately 30 minutes in the area of English. Please indicate below which of these two dates is more convenient. Also indicate the time you would like me to come into your room.

Please hand in a Lesson Plan a day earlier. Include Aim, Motivation, Procedures, etc. Indicate also past and future learnings touching this lesson.

After this lesson we will hold a post-observation conference during your preparation period. If you would like to meet me prior to your lesson, please let me know.

Sincerely,

_____

V. DiAngelo, Principal

DATES: May 6
       May 8

MY PREFERENCE IS _____ at _____ A.M./P.M.

Letter 3–36: OBSERVATION OF LESSONS—REPORT

Report of Lesson Observed

Mrs. Morris   Class 1A

Dear Mrs. Morris:

Please read this report of your lesson given on October 17.

If you wish to discuss this report before signing it, let me know. A copy will be placed in your file.

Sincerely,

_____

V. DiAngelo, Principal

Lesson Summary _____

_____

_____

Commendable Features _____

_____

_____

Suggestions for Improvement _____

_____

_____

_____

I have read and received a copy of this lesson observation.

_____

Teacher's Signature

_____

Date

Letter 3–37: OBSERVATION OF LESSONS—WEAKNESSES

TO: Mr. Mistretta, Class 5A
FR: V. DiAngelo, Principal
RE: Checklist of Lesson Weaknesses

Your lesson contained several weaknesses. I do not want to write a formal observation on this lesson. I'm sure you can do better and I would like to reschedule at a mutually convenient time. In planning your next lesson, please pay special attention to the weaknesses I have checked.

<u>Examples of weaknesses:</u>

_____ The aim did not become clear until the middle of the lesson.

_____ The pupils, working in groups, did not seem to know the purpose of their activities.

_____ There was no way of determining whether the aim had been achieved.

_____ Most pupils were inactive during the lesson.

_____ Pupils addressed all answers to the teacher.

_____ Pupils often answered in concert or called out answers.

_____ Some pupils could not answer the teacher's questions.

_____ The teacher repeated pupil answers.

_____ The teacher took too long to distribute the materials.

_____ The demonstration was not visible in the rear of the room.

_____ The bell rang for lunch before the lesson could be completed.

_____ The content was too simple for the brighter pupils.

_____ In general, pupils gave one-word or two-word answers.

_____ The teacher talked too much.

_____ The pupils were orderly but passive.

_____ Pupil reports sounded as if they had been copied from a book.

_____ The teacher wrote extensive material on the chalkboard which pupils copied in their notebooks.

_____
Principal

Letter 3–38: SUBSTITUTE TEACHERS—
CONTINGENCY PLAN

TO: Regular Teachers
RE: Contingency Plan

Class _____ Teacher _____

Date _____ Update _____ Update _____ Update _____ Update _____

Reading Groups:

Name _____ Book _____

activities _____

_____

Name _____ Book _____

activities _____

_____

Name _____ Book _____

activities _____

Mathematics Groups:

Name _____ Book _____

activities _____

Name _____ Book _____

activities _____

Social Studies Topic _____

activity _____

materials _____

Additional Activities suitable for:

class _____ group _____ Topic _____

Material _____

class _____ group _____ Topic _____

Material _____

class _____ group _____ Topic _____

Material _____

Special Programs (Remedial Reading, Speech, Gifted etc.)

Student _____ day ____ time ____ Teacher _____ Rm ____

Student _____ day ____ time ____ Teacher _____ Rm ____

Student _____ day ____ time ____ Teacher _____ Rm ____

Student _____ day ____ time ____ Teacher _____ Rm ____

Letter 3–39: SUBSTITUTE TEACHERS—GUIDE

TO: Regular Teacher
RE: Guide for the Substitute

Class _____ Teacher _____

1. The grade leader is _____ Room _____

2. Assembly day is _____ Time _____

3. Gym Periods are: Day _____ Time _____

    Day _____ Time _____

    Day _____ Time _____

4. Special Periods are: _____ Day _____ Time ____ Rm ____

    _____ Day _____ Time ____ Rm ____

    _____ Day _____ Time ____ Rm ____

    _____ Day _____ Time ____ Rm ____

5. School Session:

    Begins at _____ Students arrive _____

    Lunch period is from _____ to _____

    Students leave _____

    Afternoon session begins at _____

    Students are _____

    School session ends at _____

    Students leave _____

    The exit for this room is _____

6. The following students use the school bus:

_____   _____

_____   _____

_____   _____

They arrive at _____   They are dismissed at _____

7. The following monitors leave the room:

_____ at _____ _____ at _____

_____ at _____ _____ at _____

_____ at _____ _____ at _____

8. The following students pick up younger children:

_____ at _____ _____ at _____

_____ at _____ _____ at _____

9. The following children are picked up by older students:

_____ by _____ class _____

_____ by _____ class _____

_____ by _____ class _____

Letter 3–40: SUBSTITUTE TEACHERS—LOG

TO: Substitute Teacher
RE: Substitute Teacher Log

Class _____ Date _____

1. My name is: _____

2. Dates of coverage: _____

3. Curriculum areas of instruction:

   Reading: _____

   _____

   Math: _____

   _____

   Language Arts: _____

   _____

   Other: _____

   _____

4. Special activities: _____

5. Homework assigned: _____

6. Homework checked: _____

7. These pupils were especially helpful: _____

8. These pupils were problems (be specific): _____

   _____

9. Materials or notices distributed or collected: _____

   _____

10. Comments: _____

    _____

    _____

Letter 3–41: SUBSTITUTE TEACHERS—
REPORT TO REGULAR TEACHER

TO: Substitute Teacher
RE: Substitute's Report to Teacher

Substitute's Name _____ Class _____

Absent Teacher's Name _____ Date _____
(Please return this report to the secretary before you leave today.) Please record a summary of today's program with the class. Include all curriculum areas. Indicate if the content was your plan or the plan the teacher left.
READING   State: 1. Group Name 2. Lesson Content 3. Materials Used

_____

_____

MATHEMATICS   State: 1. Group Name 2. Lesson Content 3. Materials Used

_____

_____

LANGUAGE ARTS   State: 1. Group or Class 2. Lesson Content 3. Materials Used

Spelling _____

_____

Creative Writing _____

_____

Mechanics of Writing _____

_____

Handwriting _____

SOCIAL STUDIES   State: 1. Group or Class 2. Lesson Content 3. Materials Used

_____

_____

HOMEWORK ASSIGNED _____

Attendance: _____ Boys _____ Girls

absent A.M. _____ _____   absent P.M. _____ _____

Letter 3–42: SUBSTITUTE TEACHERS— RESPONSIBILITIES

TO: Substitute Teachers
RE: Substitute's Responsibilities

To enable each child to pursue his/her education as smoothly and completely as possible in the absence of the regular teacher, the substitute's responsibility is to:

- Notify the office immediately should a student become ill or an accident occur
- Notify the office immediately if disciplinary assistance is needed
- Consult the secretary for supplies not available in the room
- Become familiar with audio-visual materials and machines
- Report damage of equipment or materials to the office

At the end of the teaching day, the substitute should:

- Leave the teacher's desk and room in order
- Return equipment to the proper place(s)
- Turn off lights, close windows or doors
- Leave keys and materials in the office
- Check with the secretary to see if services will be needed the next day
- Make certain time sheet has been signed
- If possible, leave comments and record of day's progress and assignments completed

A substitute teacher whose services will extend more than ten (10) days should attend faculty meetings.

A substitute teacher should recognize that he or she will benefit by:

- Considering all records confidential
- Avoiding discussion and comparison of situations in one school while serving in another
- Avoiding comment on the progress of pupils or the work of the teacher
- Making all observations, suggestions or criticisms to the principal of the school involved
- Using discretion in expressing personal reactions and opinions about what is seen and heard in a classroom

Letter 3-43: EVALUATION—AUDIO-VISUAL

TO: Teachers
RE: Audio-Visual Use Evaluation

We would like to determine which pieces of equipment you find to be most useful to you in the classroom. Please consider your response carefully. Your input will help in determining what purchases we will make in the future. Place an X in the proper boxes below.

	Used more than 10 times	Used a few times	Used hardly at all
1. Overhead projector	—	—	—
2. Cassette tape recorder	—	—	—
3. Filmstrip projector	—	—	—
4. VCR	—	—	—
5. 16mm projector	—	—	—
6. 8mm projector	—	—	—
7. Opaque projector	—	—	—
8. Instamatic cameras	—	—	—
9. Record players	—	—	—
10. Slide projector	—	—	—
11. Television	—	—	—
12. Language master	—	—	—
13. Listening centers	—	—	—
14. Small prima viewers	—	—	—
15. Other A-V equipment (specify)	—	—	—

16. Additional information you feel may help to evaluate our A.V. operation _____

Letter 3–44: EVALUATION—FIELD TRIP

TO: All Teachers
RE: Field Trip Evaluation

Directions: Please rate the following field trips with a check (√) and answer the questions below.

	Fair	Good	Very Good	Excellent
1. Sixth Grade Trips				
1. Environmental park				
2. Childrens museum				
3. Ecological site				
4. State legislature				
5. Wildlife preserve				

2. Which trip most closely adhered to curriculum objectives?

3. Which trips do you feel should be continued? _____

_____

4. Of the ones not selected, which ones do you feel might be upgraded enough to retain—if any? _____

_____

5. How do you rate the conduct of students on these trips?

6. Do you feel the number of field trips is adequate? Should there be more or less?
   Adequate _____ More _____ Less _____

7. If the school budget were cut, what priority would you give field trips in relation to other activities? Explain why.

8. How do you rate the transportation provided?

9. Where would you like to go next year?

10. What support service can the school provide?

_____   _____   _____
Name   Class   Date

Letter 3–45: EVALUATION—INSERVICE TRAINING

TO: All Teachers
FR: V. DiAngelo, Principal
RE: Inservice Training

A great deal of time and money has been spent on the inservice training of our teachers. I would like to get your opinion on how successful these programs have been. Please take a few minutes to fill out this evaluation. Any comments or suggestions you make will be useful.

	Very high rating	High rating	Average rating	Need to improve
1. Information activities presented by department areas rather than mass faculty meetings.	—	—	—	—
2. The format of Tuesday's lunch, with some information presentation.	—	—	—	—
3. The amount of time allotted for individual room preparation, etc.	—	—	—	—

Individual Presentations

	Very high rating	High rating	Average rating	Need to improve
4. Math objectives and profiles.	—	—	—	—
5. English-Reading objectives and profiles.	—	—	—	—
6. Advancement on salary schedule.	—	—	—	—
7. Experiential methodology.	—	—	—	—
8. Student aide program.	—	—	—	—
9. Big Sister-Big Brother program.	—	—	—	—
10. Mass immunization.	—	—	—	—
11. Which presentation was most valuable to you?	—	—	—	—
12. Which presentation was least valuable to you?	—	—	—	—
13. Are there any suggestions you wish to add that will help us to improve the inservice program?	—	—	—	—

Letter 3–46: EVALUATION—KINDERGARTEN

KINDERGARTEN EVALUATION SHEET

Name _____ Date of Birth _____

Home Address _____ Apt. # _____

Telephone # _____

 The following items are some of the expectations of accomplishment for the child in the kindergarten. All children may not have reached the same level of growth. Please check (√) only those items in which the child has demonstrated proficiency.

Social Development	**Oct.**	**May**
1. Knows official first and last name.	____	____
2. Knows home address.	____	____
3. Recognizes community helpers; e.g., police officers, firefighters, mail carriers.	____	____
4. Knows names of adults in his home.	____	____
5. Knows and uses names of adults in classroom.	____	____
6. Identifies self as boy or girl.	____	____
7. Likes school.	____	____
8. Attends school regularly.	____	____
9. Makes friends in school.	____	____
10. Exercises reasonable self-control.	____	____
11. Demonstrates self-confidence.	____	____
12. Uses forms of polite usage; e.g., please, thank you.	____	____
13. Follows school routines.	____	____
14. Speaks freely to peers and familiar adults in school.	____	____
15. Knows names of other children in class.	____	____
16. Plays constructively alone.	____	____
17. Plays constructively with other children.	____	____

	Oct.	May
18. Is aware of the rights of other children.	——	——
19. Shares materials with classmates.	——	——
20. Adapts to changes in room and in curriculum.	——	——

Intellectual Development

	Oct.	May
1. Expresses curiosity.	——	——
2. Thinks critically.	——	——
3. Recognizes and names objects in classroom.	——	——
4. Names and groups things that go together; e.g., cup and saucer.	——	——
5. Sees likenesses and differences in shapes, sizes, colors.	——	——
6. Has developed certain concepts: up, down.	——	——
7. Identifies common sounds; e.g., clapping, peoples' voices, auto horns.	——	——
8. Listens and responds to music.	——	——
9. Enjoys stories, picture books, verse.	——	——
10. Consistently holds picture book right side up.	——	——
11. Uses equipment and materials for constructive purposes.	——	——
12. Builds creatively with blocks.	——	——
a. Alone b. With other children	——	——
13. Participates in dramatic play.	——	——
14. Likes to draw, paint, paste, etc.	——	——
15. Speaks in sentences.	——	——
16. Relates ideas in logical sequence; retells stories.	——	——
17. Pronounces sounds distinctly.	——	——
18. Shows ability to pay attention.	——	——
19. Narrates own experiences.	——	——
20. Memorizes and sings simple songs.	——	——

	Oct.	May
21. Uses descriptive adjectives.	____	____
22. Begins to develop a sight vocabulary; e.g., own name on crayon can and cubby, Helper's Chart, Weather Chart, safety signs.	____	____
23. Recognizes numerals as distinguished from letters of alphabet.	____	____
24. Follows simple series of verbal directions.	____	____
25. Displays curiosity in experimentation.	____	____
26. Asks questions of adults.	____	____
27. Recognizes nine colors: red, orange, yellow, green, blue, violet, black, white, brown.	____	____

Physical Development

	Oct.	May
1. Has satisfactory large muscle coordination.	____	____
2. Has adequate small muscle coordination.	____	____
3. Handles classroom materials with ease; e.g. scissors, manipulative toys.	____	____
4. Uses two feet alternately in going up and down stairs.	____	____
5. Fastens own shoes.	____	____

Health and Safety Habits

	Oct.	May
1. Knows correct way to cross street.	____	____
2. Knows and applies safety rules in classroom; e.g., correct way to carry chair, limit of height of block buildings.	____	____
3. Washes hands without a reminder before eating and after using toilet.	____	____
4. Tries foods strange to him.	____	____

Special Talents

_____

_____

Special Needs

_____

_____

Letter 3-47: EVALUATION—SCHEDULES

TO: All Teachers
FR: V. DiAngelo, Principal
RE: Evaluation of Schedules

We are trying to improve our school's master schedule.

Mark the column that best evaluates the progress made so far. Where you feel the question cannot be answered with a check, add your comments at the bottom. You may sign your name or remain anonymous.

Thank you.

	Fully Accomplished	Mostly Accomplished	Partly Accomplished	Not Accomplished
1. To provide a one-half hour lunch period for teachers and students.	___	___	___	___
2. To eliminate unnecessary teacher supervision of study hall, cafeteria, restroom, school grounds, etc.	___	___	___	___
3. To increase the amount of instructional time offered students by shortening homeroom sessions.	___	___	___	___
4. To cut down on the number of different rooms any one teacher has to go to.	___	___	___	___
5. To provide double block sessions for Art, Industrial Art, Home Economics and Music.	___	___	___	___
6. To increase the number of cocurricular activity time slots by two each week.	___	___	___	___
7. To insure that no student has more than one study hall each day.	___	___	___	___
8. To free teachers so that they may be available for students who need extra help.	___	___	___	___
9. To provide a common meeting time for departments.	___	___	___	___
10. To standardize a number of existing complex rotations.	___	___	___	___

Comments: _____

_____

_____

Letter 3-48: EVALUATION—TRIP

TO: Teachers Planning a Trip
FR: V. DiAngelo, Principal
RE: Trip Evaluation Report

<u>Planning the Trip</u>

- Clear all visits with museums whether for guided or unguided tours. Check for admission fees, days and hours museum is open to groups, lunchroom facilities, prices of soft drinks or lunches, etc.
- Investigate the trip site beforehand, especially if no guide is available. Refer to trip folder or teacher who has made the trip before.

TRIP EVALUATION REPORT

Place visited: _____ Date: _____

Appropriate grade level: _____

Highlights: _____

_____

_____

Curriculum area reinforced: _____

Problems encountered: _____

_____

_____

Guided tour available: Yes _____ No _____

Lunch facilities (type): _____

_____
Teacher's Signature

Letter 3-49: EVALUATION—VOLUNTEERS

TO: Selected Teachers
RE: Teacher's Evaluation of Volunteer

General:

    Is the volunteer always punctual to class?
    Does the volunteer attend class regularly?

Approach:

1. Does your volunteer show impatience toward students?

2. How does she/he work with you in planning and teaching?

3. Does she/he take sides during a disagreement between the teacher and students?

4. Does she/he tend to give you the idea that she/he enjoys her/his work or does she/he give you the idea that she/he has to do it?

5. What is the volunteer's reaction to outbreaks of violence in the class?

Ability:

6. How does she/he handle the class when the teacher is absent or while momentarily taking over?

7. What kinds of methods does your volunteer employ in teaching students?

8. How much success does the volunteer have in motivating a student?

9. Does the volunteer make it easier for the students to understand the work when they are in doubt? If so, how?

10. Is the volunteer too forceful or not forceful enough toward the students?

11. What was the main job of your volunteer? Did he fulfill this job as best he could?

12. Can your volunteer work with any type of student? (slow, fast, black, white, etc.)

13. Do you think that your volunteer should be one of the fall volunteers?

Miscellaneous:

14. Would you have any objection to having this paper read by your volunteer?

    Thank you,

    _____
    V. DiAngelo, Principal

Teacher's Name _____   Comments _____

Volunteer's Name _____   _____

Subject _____   _____

Letter 3–50: REFERRING STUDENTS—ACCIDENT REPORT

ACCIDENT REPORT

Please report accidents to the office immediately. This report must be turned in on the same day as the accident. Teachers of early childhood grades will fill out this form for the child.

Pupil's Name: _____ Class: _____

Home Address: _____ Phone: _____

Date of Accident: _____ Time: _____

Description of Accident: _____

_____

_____

Description of Injury: _____

_____

_____

What was the pupil doing at the time of the accident? _____

_____

Name and title of person supervising the pupil at time of accident:

_____

Name of witness: # 1 _____

           # 2 _____
Attach statements of witnesses.

Describe nature of first aid provided: _____

Was parent notified? _____ How? _____ Time: _____

Statement of Custodian, if appropriate: _____

Was ambulance or private physician called? _____ Supply details: _____

_____

Statement of School Supervisor: _____

_____

_____

Letter 3–51: REFERRING STUDENTS—ANECDOTAL DATA

ANECDOTAL DATA FORM

School _____ Principal _____

Pupil's Name _____ Teacher _____

Note: In an effort to get the necessary support service to assist troubled pupils we must maintain careful anecdotal records. The following simple-to-maintain form should be used to document untoward or bizarre behavior of pupils. Keep a separate form for each child you are monitoring. In the third column describe the incident without being judgmental.

DATE	ACTIVITY	DESCRIPTION OF INCIDENT OR INTERVIEW

Letter 3–52: REFERRING STUDENTS—DISCIPLINARY ACTION

TO: All Professional Employees Assigned to P.S. 54
FROM: V. DiAngelo, Principal
SUBJECT: Referral of Students to Administrators for Disciplinary Action
DATE: December 1, 19XX

I would like to clarify what happens when a student is referred to the administration for discipline.

Teachers should usually handle their own discipline problems, including necessary punishment. At times, because of the seriousness of the offense or for a variety of other reasons, the teacher prefers to refer the student to an administrator.

The administrator will await the teacher's report before taking action. Then, however, the referral is total. The disposition of the case will be made on the professional judgment of the administrator, after consulting the teacher. The administrator's decision will be based on the total school record of the student, as well as his record in a given teacher's class. What may appear to be a minor offense to a given teacher may be considered more serious when viewed by an administrator examining the total pattern.

The teacher will be informed as to what happened. The main goal is to help the student improve.

Letter 3–53: REFERRING STUDENTS—GIFTED STUDENTS

TO: Kindergarten Teachers
RE: Checklist for Identifying Gifted Pupils

We are trying to identify those pupils who would benefit from placement in a Gifted Grade One Class.

Class: _____ Date: _____ Teacher: _____

When compared with other children in the Kindergarten, which of your pupils possess, to a marked degree, some of the following characteristics? Be particularly observant of the youngest children in the class. Do not exclude any child because of a speech defect.

1. Has unusually good vocabulary.
2. Has ideas which are often very original in one or more areas (i.e., block play, free activities, art, rhythms, sharing).
3. Is alert, keenly observant; responds quickly.
4. Has an unusually good memory.
5. Has a long attention span.
6. Recognizes, on his own, some words in books on the browsing table.
7. Uses longer sentences.
8. Reasons things out; thinks clearly, recognizes relationships, comprehends meanings.
9. Is curious about many activities and places outside immediate environment and/or experience.
10. Is a leader in several kinds of activities. Is able to influence others to work toward desirable goals.
11. Has outstanding talent in special area(s) such as art, music, rhythms, dramatics. (Indicate area(s) of talent.)
12. Other.

If you have any pupils who exhibit at least three of the above characteristics, please list their names below. Following each name, list the number of all characteristics that fit the pupil. You may have only one or two such children—or none. Use the spaces below:

Pupil's Name	Characteristics (indicate by #)
1. _____	_____
2. _____	_____
3. _____	_____

_____
Signature

Letter 3–54: REFERRING STUDENTS— PUPIL PROMOTION PROFILE

TO: CLASSROOM TEACHERS
RE: PUPIL PROMOTION PROFILE

Pupil's Name: _____ Class: _____ Date: _____

Address: _____ Phone: _____ Birthdate: _____

Reading Scores: _____ Date of Test: _____ Functional Level: _____

Math Scores: _____ Date of Test: _____ Functional Level: _____

Strengths Noted by Teacher: _____

_____

_____

Weaknesses Noted by Teacher: _____

_____

_____

Written English level as noted by Teacher: Above _____ On _____ Below _____ Level

Common errors made in written work: _____

_____

Physical limitations, if any: _____

Speech problems: _____

Attendance: _____ Lateness: _____

Work Habits: _____

Personal and Social Adjustment: _____

Out-of-School Factors: _____

Parent Contact during day: _____ in evening: _____

Siblings in school, and class: _____

Comments: _____

_____

Letter 3–55: REFERRING STUDENTS—REFERRAL FORM

REFERRAL FORM

Name of Child: _____ Date of Birth: _____

Class: _____ Teacher: _____ Date of Referral: _____

Reason for Referral:

Steps taken by teacher:

Contacts with home made by teacher:

Comments made by other school personnel (if appropriate):

Academic work:

Comments or notations made by previous teachers:

_____
Teacher's Signature

Letter 3–56: REFERRING STUDENTS—REFERRAL FORM

REFERRAL FORM

NAME (Last, First) _____ Section _____ Teacher _____

Time Sent _____ Period _____ Date _____ Subject _____

Grades Last Six Weeks _____ This Six Weeks _____
(Where Applicable)

Please Check

____ Failure to conform to   ____ Lunch Conduct   ____ Smoking
     class procedures

____ Disrespectful   ____ Hall Conduct   ____ Other (Explain)

____ Willful disobedience   ____ Fighting

To Be Completed in Office—Action Taken

____ Conference with   ____ Parent Conference   ____ Excluded from
     student   class

____ Detention   ____ Referred to   ____ Suspended
                                         counselor

____ Called parent   ____ Referred to   ____ Other (Explain)
                                         Pupil Services

Letter 3–57: REFERRING STUDENTS—WEEKLY REPORT

To: _____ Date _____

From: Principal

Subject: Weekly Report on _____

　　　　Please fill in the following form by check marks or brief comments and return it to my office before 3 P.M. Friday.

1. How many absences this week? _____ latenesses? _____

2. Is he/she getting to class on time? Yes _____ No _____

　　Comment _____

3. Does pupil have books and materials every day? Yes _____ No _____

　　Comment: _____

4. Are assignments completed? _____

　　Comment: _____

5. Is attention paid in class? Yes _____ No _____

　　Comment: _____

6. Does pupil contribute to discussions? Yes _____ No _____

　　Comment: _____

7. Grades Received: Project Work _____

　　　　　　　　　　Daily Quizzes _____

　　　　　　　　　　Unit Tests _____

　　　　　　　　　　Other _____

8. Describe briefly his/her attitude _____

_____

_____

Teacher's Signature

Letter 3–58: ADMINISTRATIVE—CALENDAR

TO: All Teachers
FR: V. DiAngelo, Principal

END-OF-TERM CALENDAR

Please read through this calendar in advance so that you will be able to anticipate what has to be done.

- Observe all due dates; there can be no time extensions.
- Pupils are to receive worthwhile instruction through June 24.
- Check off each item on the calendar as it is completed.
- Be sure that all entries are neat, complete, accurate, and appropriate. Do not allow pupils to see record cards.
- If you have a trip planned on the day when material is to be collected, please see that it is collected the day before.
- Do not give out any advance information as to class or teacher.
- Leave room decorations up until June 22.

June

4–First clerical half-day. Children excused for P.M. session. Hot lunch served at 11:30 A.M. No refunds if absent.

5–Promotion sheets due in main office. Sixth grade teachers send office cards, class cards, test cards, and health forms for transmittal to junior high.

7–Eighth Grade teachers send in names of pupils who are deserving of attendance, service, and conduct awards.

12–"New" class cards, etc., distributed to next year's teachers.

13–Senior Class Day

17–Second clerical half-day. Children excused for P.M. session.

You will receive a copy of:
Organization of the school.
Class composition sheet for new class.

You will complete:
Address cards indicating new grade and room.
Set of office cards including Emergency Contact Card.

You should have for each child:
Cumulative Record Card
Test Record Card
Health Forms
Reading Card

18–Finish report cards. Be sure to indicate "Promoted" or "Not Promoted." Also indicate the new room to which the child is to report in September. Make sure that the date of the first day of school (Sept. 9) is on every report card.

21–Audio-visual equipment and other material must be returned to the school aides in Room 114.
Kindergarten graduation in the auditorium at 10:00 A.M.

24–Make up new roll book. Send new roll book to the office for safekeeping.
Send promotion cards to the office by 1:00 P.M.

25–Graduation in auditorium. Brothers and sisters with notes from parents will be escorted by aides to the auditorium. All class parties to be held in the afternoon.

26–Give out report cards.
Pupils dismissed at 12 Noon.
Complete old roll books.
Lock everything. Dispose of trash.
Fill out "Close of School" letter and turn in with keys.

HAVE A HAPPY AND HEALTHFUL VACATION ! ! !

Letter 3–59: ADMINISTRATIVE—CONFERENCES

STAFF CONFERENCE NOTES

Monday, November 19, 19XX

I. Administrative Notes

   1.1 Attendance Period: Third attendance period ends November 30. Total days this period: 19. Total days to date: 53.

   1.2 Health Records: Please review the health records for the pupils in your class. Check to see that any necessary referrals have been made and that all entries are complete and up to date.

   1.3 PTA Events:
   Evening meeting: Tuesday, November 20, 7:30 P.M.
   Holiday Fair: Tuesday, December 4, Gym.
   Holiday Show (Puppets): Wednesday, December 12.
   Kindergarten Show: Tuesday, December 18.

   1.4 Traffic Safety: Please give lessons on proper crossing of streets. Stress the dangers of mid-block crossing, crossing where there is no guard, etc. In the lower grades, integrate this with your map and chart skills.

   1.5 Science: You will soon receive a notice giving details of our Science Fair, which will take place the first week of February. Begin planning now for group and individual projects.

   1.6 Literary Magazine: Please be sure that you are sending children's work to your grade leader on a regular basis. All teachers should be using the tally sheets distributed earlier this year.

II. Supervision and Improvement of Instruction

   2.1 Homework: Please review the circular distributed in September. Homework is never to be given as punishment. School policy is not to assign homework over weekends.

   2.2 Bulletin Boards: Classroom bulletin boards are an effective way of vitalizing learning. Be sure that they are changed regularly to reflect current work. Also, make sure that all children have a chance sometime during the year to have at least one item displayed.

   2.3 Math Activity Cards: Mrs. Bartone has prepared a series of 30 activity cards for intermediate grades in math. These self-directed cards provide fast-working pupils with some stimulating activity when they finish their classwork ahead of the others.

   2.4 Questioning: An analysis of recent classroom observation reveals that many teachers can improve their techniques of questioning. We will discuss this at our grade level conferences. Be certain that you ask a balance of thought and fact questions.

   2.5 Plan Books: In planning your week's work, give some attention to the teaching of skills in the area of physical education. Some teachers are merely providing their pupils with free play.

Letter 3-60: ADMINISTRATIVE—CONFERENCES

TO: All Teachers
FR: V. DiAngelo, Principal
RE: Parent-Teacher Conferences

As we get ready for this year's parent-teacher conferences, it is good for us all to consider how the conferences can be most helpful in our common effort to improve the child's achievement.

When a parent comes to us for a conference, we can be sure that he or she wants to talk with us about the child. The parent will be encouraged when we listen carefully and actively and when we treat him or her with courtesy and respect.

It is good to be prepared for a conference with a parent. The conference will be successful if we review the child's school records; talk with other school personnel such as guidance counselors, other teachers, etc.; have the child's work folders available; have ratings available; plan what we want to tell the parent and jot down the information on a file card so that we can refresh our memory before we speak to a parent.

Smiling when greeting a parent is a fine way to begin a conference. Positive comments should be made first. Every child has many fine qualities we can mention. But we should not do all the talking. We need to get the parent to talk. If we feel that a plan of action is needed to help the child improve, the parent's cooperation is important. The conference should end on a positive note just as it began. It should hold out an opportunity for further communication about the child.

Because a conference is a way to help the child learn more effectively, we need to make a few notes to summarize what was said, and then to follow through on any ideas the parent and we have agreed on.

There are some basic hints that are generally conducive to good conferences. Some of these are:

- Be prepared.
- Keep faith with the child. No "tales out of school."
- Discourage comparisons with sisters or brothers or other children.
- Listen attentively to what parents say. Allow parents time to be self-expressive.
- Praise, but don't flatter. Flattery is false and easily detected. Praise is sincere and its message includes the worthy qualities which each child has.
- Avoid argument.
- Show empathy. Place yourself in the parent's shoes.
- Don't preach at parents.
- Avoid jargon. Speak in simple, clear terms.
- Be frank but don't be blunt. How you tell is as important as what you tell.
- Keep avenues of communication open.

You have my best wishes for successful conferences. Let me know if I can help.

Letter 3–61: ADMINISTRATIVE—CONFERENCES

TO: Teachers
FR: V. DiAngelo, Principal
RE: Techniques for Improving Parent-Teacher Conferences/Interviews

Parent-Teacher Conferences/Interviews are an important way to build strong home-school ties. Listed below are techniques for preparing for, conducting, and following up an interview.

1. Remember, while conducting the interview, that it is a conversation with a purpose.

2. Rapport between the parent and the teacher is most important in laying the foundation for a successful interview. It is up to the teacher to conduct a successful interview.

3. Prior to the actual interview, assemble all the materials you need, such as marking books, rating sheets, tests, and samples of class work.

4. Welcome every parent warmly. Make each one feel at ease and secure. (Many parents, when they are summoned to or come to school, feel uneasy, guilty, timid, threatened, and a sense of failure.)

5. Do not sit behind your desk. It is far easier to build a cooperative, workable relationship if you are seated alongside the parent. Behind the desk, the teacher is in a position of authority, not partnership.

6. Open the interview on a positive note. Use expressions of approval, praise, or satisfaction for something the child can do well or has experienced with success. Such an approach draws the school and home closer together since the parent has a right to hear both the pleasant and unpleasant things about a child's work and behavior.

7. Do not at any time refer to a child or his/her pattern of behavior in these terms: liar, stupid, dumb, delinquent, or lazy. Describe some of the things the child does and let the parents come to their own conclusions: "John does not finish his work" or "Mary acts as though she doesn't hear any instructions."

8. Hold the conference in a quiet place, free from interruptions.

9. Accept the parent and his/her explanations without showing surprise or disapproval. If you do this, you will get a true and honest picture of the parent's feelings and attitudes.

10. Never argue with a parent or allow emotions to enter into the interview. It will hinder your usefulness rather than help the situation.

11. Be brief but not curt in your interview. Many parents will want to talk to you. If a parent seems to require too much time, suggest that he/she return to see you at a time convenient for both.

12. Remember that there will be other parents present and perhaps within hearing. Therefore, do not get involved with emotional or confidential materials.

13. Listen to the parent, encourage him/her to talk, and then listen to what he/she has to say.

14. Be sympathetic, but bear in mind that you are not a social worker, psychologist, or psychiatrist.

15. Be cautious in your advice. Do not become involved in any deep emotional situation.

16. Close the interview on a constructive, pleasant, or positive note, such as a statement of a plan for cooperative action in helping and guiding the child.

Letter 3-62: ADMINISTRATIVE—FREE PERIOD

TO: Principal   Date: _____

FROM: _____ Class: _____

SUBJECT: Notice of Missed Preparation (Free) Period

       This is to inform you that I missed my scheduled preparation period as indicated below:

Date: _____   I hereby request:

Period: _____   ____ A Makeup Prep

Cluster Teacher: _____   ____ Payroll Compensation

              Teacher's Signature: _____

- -

| Date: |
| Period: |

DISPOSITION

I have received a makeup prep for the above.

           Teacher's Signature _____

           Date: _____

The above was entered for payroll compensation on _____
                                           Date

           Secretary's Signature: _____

Letter 3–63: ADMINISTRATIVE—HOMEWORK

TO: Teachers
FR: V. DiAngelo, Principal
RE: Homework Criteria

There is no rigid policy regarding the matter of homework because of varying conditions in schools and homes. Worthwhile homework assignments can extend lessons begun in the classroom, build independent study habits, and encourage children to think and work creatively outside of school. On the other hand, it is doubtful whether giving large amounts of homework is an important and useful means of promoting educational growth in elementary school children. The following guidelines and criteria for homework assignments take into account mental health, as well as intellectual aspects. Observance of these principles will make homework more effective and profitable.

Criteria for Homework Assignments

When considering homework assignments, the following considerations are important:

1. Does the assignment serve a valid educational purpose?

2. Is the assignment reasonable and consistent with the child's abilities, needs, and interests?

3. Does the homework assignment interfere with other worthwhile activities in which the child might engage while out of school?

4. Will the assignment extend the child's knowledge without fostering discouragement and resentment?

5. Does the pupil understand what is to be done? Is the assignment clear?

6. Is the length of the assignment reasonable—a maximum of thirty minutes for primary and one hour for intermediate grades?

7. Use the form below to send home homework to pupils absent for three or more days.

TEACHER _____ DATE _____

STUDENT _____

HOMEWORK FOR (NUMBER OF DAYS) _____

ASSIGNMENT IS: _____

_____

_____

_____

_____

_____

Parent's Signature

Letter 3–64: ADMINISTRATIVE—HOMEWORK

TO: Classroom Teachers
FR: V. DiAngelo, Principal
RE: Homework Guidelines

1. Make homework attractive in itself; do not use it for punishment.
2. Try a variety of carefully planned approaches that stimulate, interest, and actively involve your students.
3. Accept student criticism and encourage students to help in planning assignments that are relevant and motivating.
4. Do not let homework make unreasonable demands on students. Our school policy suggests the following allotments by grade level (summarized):

Grade	Daily Homework
1	0–15 minutes
2–5	20–35 minutes
6–8	40–90 minutes

5. Use completed homework for additional educational purposes once in a while: display original homework endeavors, set up a learning center in which students can scrutinize and use each other's after-school accomplishments, or have each student keep (and periodically evaluate) his or her own homework log.

Note:

Do you give homework? You probably should, in moderation. One study showed that 80 percent of all students want it; yet 50 percent feel uneasy about the nature and amount they are receiving.

The best teachers do not necessarily give the most homework, but they do give more unusual work. This includes assignments for those who want them (and all will if it's something exciting!), assignments offering students a say in what will be done, and assignments that spark creativity.

Letter 3–65: ADMINISTRATIVE—HOMEWORK

TO: All Teachers
FR: V. DiAngelo, Principal
RE: Homework Policy

An important part of your work involves assigning, checking, and evaluating homework assignments. This policy statement will help you plan meaningful and varied homework assignments.

Homework's purpose is to:

1. reinforce what the child has been taught in school by:
   - providing practice of a learned skill
   - extending interest
   - extending knowledge
   - providing practice in researching information
   - providing drill in weak areas
2. developing positive attitudes towards school
3. developing good work/study habits
4. encouraging creative activities beyond basic requirements

Homework in the elementary school should:

1. serve a useful purpose
2. be related to classroom instruction
3. be within the ability of the child to accomplish
4. be individualized for those who need this type of reinforcement
5. be given daily
6. be checked by the teacher <u>daily</u>
7. never be given as:
   - punishment
   - busywork

Homework assignments should follow these guidelines:

1. grade one: no formal homework
2. grade two: written homework
3. in all grades: home study is encouraged
4. grades four through eight: home study from texts is to be emphasized

Parental responsibility regarding homework requires that a parent:

1. check homework daily
2. confer with teacher if child is unclear about assignment
3. show interest
4. take assignments as a serious matter
5. answer questions
6. assist in planning time
7. provide proper atmosphere
8. remove distractions: i.e., radio/TV/music
9. provide necessary supplies
10. save magazines for reference
11. look at finished assignment for:
    - neatness
    - accuracy
    - completeness
12. listen to youngster

Letter 3–66: ADMINISTRATIVE—PREFERENCE

PREFERENCE SHEET

Date: _____

Teacher's Name _____

(In listing class, use 2–1 to signify top class in Second Grade, or 3–4 to signify bottom class in Third Grade, etc.)

(Check One)

	Grade	Difficult (3 or 4)	Less Difficult (1 or 2)
Present Class (19XX-XX)	____	_____	_____
Class 19XX-XX	____	_____	_____
Class 19XX-XX	____	_____	_____

Grade Preference
for 19XX-XX   1. ____   2. ____   3. ____ (Three Different Choices)

Leaves taken during past three years: Date: _____

Duration: _____

Do you expect to be at P.S. 54 next year? _____

Comments: _____

_____

_____

_____
Teacher's Signature

Place this completed form in my mail box. Please understand that where it is advisable and possible, such preferences will be honored. You may, of course, discuss your request with me at any time.

_____
V. DiAngelo, Principal

REQUEST FOR SUPPLIES

Teacher _____ Class _____ Room _____

       Please plan ahead for the supplies you need. Supplies will be distributed every other month except for emergency items.

	Sept.	Nov.	Jan.	March	May
Paper 8× 10 white lined					
6×9 yellow					
Rulers					
Eraser					
Construction Paper					
Chalk					
Duplicating Paper					
Photocopy Paper					

Filled (Aide Initials) _____

Received (Teacher Initials) _____

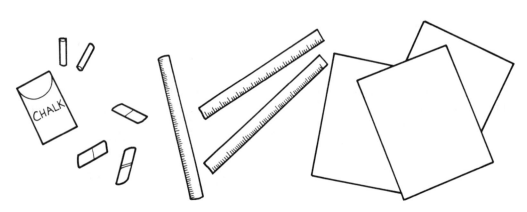

Letter 3–68: PERSONAL LETTER—ACHIEVEMENT

April 11, 19XX

Mrs. Van Houten
Teacher, Class 2C

Dear Mrs. Van Houten:

Please accept my congratulations on a job well done! The fine showing of your pupils on the math achievement test is a credit to your devotion and talent. Their achievement would not have been possible without your encouragement and hard work.

So many of your colleagues have mentioned your class' showing to me with a feeling of shared pride and professional admiration. Many parents of pupils in your class have taken this occasion to tell me how pleased they are to have you as their child's teacher.

All of us at P.S. 54 respect you as a professional and warm human being. It is nice to know that the parents also recognize your varied abilities as this performance attests. I am so proud of you!

Sincerely,

_____

V. DiAngelo, Principal

Letter 3-69: PERSONAL LETTER—APPRECIATION

December 18, 19XX

Miss Adamson
Music Teacher

Dear Miss Adamson:

I would like to thank you for the many hours you put in on the holiday play. I was very impressed with the songs, which had your imprint on them. It was carefully planned, professionally executed, and well received.

Your high standards and exemplary performance are among our school's greatest assets. I frequently point your work out as an example for our new teachers to emulate.

I particularly like the way in which you _____

_____

_____

Again, a hearty thank-you for an outstanding job. I hope you and your family enjoy a well-deserved holiday vacation. We are so fortunate to have you at P.S. 54.

Sincerely,

_____
V. DiAngelo, Principal

Letter 3–70: PERSONAL LETTER—PRAISE

September 30, 19XX

Mrs. Kinny
Teacher, Class 6C

Dear Mrs. Kinny:

   On Tuesday evening, September 28, after a long and difficult day, you attended a meeting of the Parent Association of P.S. 54. You made yourself available to the parents both during the meeting and afterwards at the coffee and cake social.

   This type of activity contributes to the public relations image of the school. It gave the parents of the community an opportunity to meet you and speak with you. You have helped us to impress the parents with our outstanding programs and staff.

   Thank you for your efforts.

Sincerely,

_____

V. DiAngelo, Principal

I have read this letter and understand
that it will be placed in my file.

_____

Teacher's Signature

cc: Teacher

Letter 3–71: PERSONAL LETTER—RECOMMENDATION

March 22, 19XX

To Whom It May Concern:

Joan Smith is a superlative teacher who gave our school nine years of dedicated service. Her teaching methods have produced knowledgeable, enthusiastic, and grateful students. I have had the pleasure of sitting in on some of her class discussions and became so captivated that I simply could not leave. Her students were prepared for these discussions in a variety of ways: through special assignments, homework guidelines, small-group discussions, library visits, etc.—and the depth of understanding they exhibited was astounding!

Mrs. Smith is an advocate of small groupings, and never seems to run out of good ideas. She may, for example, "prime" several students to instruct a few classmates, line up student teams for a major project, or initiate peer drill sessions for memorizing and reviewing important material before a test.

She also gives special attention to the individuals in her classes, frequently working on one-to-one basis with them. She even created an individualized program to supplement her curriculum. The core of this program consists of "fact folders" for those particularly interested in a topic, "fun quizzes" to check and reinforce knowledge, and "project suggestion cards" for creative and adventurous students. With these many opportunities available, every student finds challenging, rewarding, and often "personalized" enrichment experiences.

I consider Mrs. Smith to be one of those extraordinary educators who will always put forth a wholehearted effort . . . with amazing results! Our loss will most assuredly be your gain.

Sincerely,

_____

V. DiAngelo, Principal

Letter 3-72: PERSONAL LETTER—SYMPATHY

Dear Mildred,

All of us at P.S. 54 were saddened to learn of the loss of your husband on February 5.

This must be a very difficult time for you. If there is anything that I can do that in any way will ease these difficult days, please let me know at once.

It must have been a great comfort for George to have you as a wife. I know you were a great source of pride and admiration to your husband as you are to all of us at school.

Your many friends at P.S. 54 share my warm feelings for you and your family at this time. Please let us know if there is anything any of us can do.

Affectionately,

V. DiAngelo, Principal

SECTION
4

Letters
to
Staff Members

Letter 4–1: ADVANCED DEGREE

Dear Mr. Mistretta:

Congratulations on being granted the Master's degree in reading from Southport University.

We are all very proud of you and we recognize how much time and effort went into your preparation. I am sure the long hours of study and financial sacrifice were considerable.

Your family must be very proud of you as is the P.S. 54 family.

You will be placed on the appropriate salary step as soon as we get the enclosed Salary Differential Form filled out.

Again, congratulations and best wishes.

Sincerely,

_____

V. DiAngelo, Principal

Letter 4–2: APPLICATION FORM FOR SCHOOL EMPLOYEE

Name _____

Address _____

Social Security No. _____ Phone No. _____
In case of emergency, name and phone number of person to contact:

_____

PERSONAL DATA

    1. Do you know of any disability or communicable disease which would prevent your passing a physical examination and receiving a health card?

    _____

    2. Previous work experience: (List type of experience, dates of employment, etc.)

Employer	Location	From	To

    3. Last place of employment and date of employment:

    _____

    4. Have you ever been discharged from a position? _____ If answered "YES", please explain. (Include job title and date)

    _____

Would you be willing to substitute in Food Service? _____

When could you begin work? _____
In what area would you prefer to work?

_____

REFERENCES: (Name) (Present Address)

_____

OTHER COMMENTS:

_____

INTERVIEWED FOR: _____ DATE/TIME: _____ INITIALS: _____

DATE: _____ SIGNATURE OF APPLICANT _____

Letter 4–3: APPROACHING RETIREMENT

Dear Mrs. Morris:

We plan to honor all school employees who plan to retire this year at a luncheon on June 10.

The following resolution has been passed by the School Board. A copy of it on heavy parchment will be presented to you at that time.

RESOLVED, that the School Board hereby proclaims the third week of June of each year as a time to honor all school district employees; be it further

RESOLVED, that the members of the faculty, staff, parents, and pupils offer their sincere appreciation to all retiring staff members, many of whom have devoted many years of significant service to the children of their community; and be it further

RESOLVED, that the School Board offer their best wishes for a pleasant retirement to all staff members who are about to conclude their official relationship with our district.

Good Luck!

V. DiAngelo Principal

Letter 4–4: CUSTODIAN

TO: Custodian
RE: Request for Repairs

_____ (initials)

_____ (date)

Teacher _____ Room _____

Date _____

_____ broken shade   _____ clogged sink

_____ light bulb   _____ leaky faucet

_____ ripped window shade   _____ closet door

_____ torn shade cord   _____ wardrobe door

_____ broken window   _____ broken lock location

_____ radiator malfunction   _____

_____ other _____

Letter 4–5: CUSTODIAN

TO: All Staff Members
FROM: V. DiAngelo, Principal
RE: Custodial Operations

Please take a moment to respond to this survey of how staff members rate our custodial operations. Using a scale of 1 to 5, with 1 as "poor" and 5 as "excellent," rate each of these items.

_____ 1. Are your baskets emptied regularly?

_____ 2. Is your floor swept?

_____ 3. How would you describe the attitude of the custodial workers toward staff members?

_____ 4. What is the condition of hallways and stair wells?

_____ 5. How are the pupil and staff toilets maintained?

_____ 6. What is the cleanliness level of the lunchroom?

_____ 7. How would you describe the condition of faculty and staff rooms?

_____ 8. What is the general level of school appearance indoors?

_____ 9. What is the general level of school appearance outdoors?

10. Please make any comments you wish, below.

_____

_____

_____

Letter 4–6: EXCESSIVE ABSENCES

November 8, 19XX

Dear Mrs. Linares:

Our records indicate that you have been absent seven days since school started in September. These absences are:

_____

_____

_____

Many of these dates were Mondays and Fridays. I spoke to you about this earlier this year and sent you a letter on October 22. There has been no improvement. Please let me have, in writing, the reason for each of the absences listed above. According to District Office policy, you must now furnish a physician's verification for every day you are out.

_____

V. DiAngelo, Principal

Letter 4–7: GROUP GUIDANCE LESSON

Guidance Counselor _____

Class: _____ No. of the Session _____

Date _____ Time ____ Sex of the Group _____

COUNSELOR'S REACTION TO THE SESSION (content, process, interpersonal relationship)

CONTENT (What was discussed) _____

_____

_____

_____

_____

_____

_____

_____

PROCESS (How did it develop) _____

_____

_____

_____

_____

_____

_____

_____

INTERPERSONAL RELATIONSHIP (What is taking place with individuals including the leader)

_____

_____

Letter 4–8: GUIDANCE INTERVIEWS

TO: Staff Members
RE: Guidance Interviews
FR: V. DiAngelo, Principal

There are times when teachers, counselors, advisers, or others conduct interviews with parents, agency personnel, or others regarding a pupil in our school. In order to avoid duplication of service and to keep a record of pertinent data, I am asking all personnel to maintain the following "Record of Guidance Interview."

Date _____

Name of Child _____

Date of Birth _____ Class _____

Address _____

_____ Phone _____

Parents' Names _____

Description of Contact
(e.g., telephone call to agency, parent interview, teacher conference)

_____

_____

_____

Summary of Pertinent Facts _____

_____

_____

Letter 4–9: GROUP GUIDANCE SESSIONS

TO: Guidance Counselor
RE: Group Guidance Sessions

Counselor _____

Class _____ Date _____

Time _____

No. in Group _____ Sex of Group _____

No. of the Session _____

COUNSELOR'S NOTES:

    (a) Topic (b) Interaction (Dynamic) (c) Reactions

    (d) Future Goals _____

_____

_____

_____

_____

_____

_____

_____

_____

_____

_____

_____

_____

_____

_____

_____

Letter 4–10: HOME INSTRUCTION

TO: SUPERINTENDENT
RE: REQUEST FOR HOME INSTRUCTION FOR PUPIL
FR: V. DiAngelo, Principal

We are requesting home instruction for:

Pupil: _____ Born: _____
        Print Last Name   First

Address: _____ Zone _____ Apt. _____

Parents: _____ _____

A physician's note is enclosed _____ OR parent has note _____
Homebound teacher should confer with:

Name of school official _____ Room _____

Phone _____
For pupils above the 5th grade, please complete information below:
School Subjects pupil is taking or will be required to pass
Achievement tests in: Language, Math (be specific), Regents, Modified, etc.

1. _____ 4. _____

2. _____ 5. _____

3. _____ 6. _____
Other Items: Graduation requirements, Attendance record, Guidance File, Summer
        School, etc.

_____

_____

_____.

_____

V. DiAngelo, Principal

Letter 4-11: LAVATORY USE

TO: Faculty and Staff
FR: V. DiAngelo, Principal
RE: Lavatory Use

Because of several instances of vandalism and graffiti in the student lavatories, we are asking that you institute a new procedure regarding student use of the lavatories. While no student may ever be denied the use of lavatory facilities, it would seem necessary to institute some control over the procedure.

We are asking, therefore, that every teacher keep an "Out-of-Room Book" for those students who are issued lavatory passes, including the times out and back to the classroom. Please indicate your name and the room number for each period of the day. The book is to be turned into the office at the end of the teacher's day. People on hall duty will henceforth be required to check the lavatories for damage. If such damage is discovered, we will then be able to determine the time it happened and, thanks to your recordkeeping, narrow down the field of possible perpetrators.

I will be letting the students know of this new procedure in the hope that it may act as a deterrent to a potential vandal.

I thank you in advance for your cooperation in this matter.

Letter 4–12: LIBRARY ASSIGNMENT

TO: Librarian
RE: Library Assignment Alert Card

I have given my students the following library research assignment: _____
_____

Could you please have appropriate materials on hand and accessible—specifically including the following:

_____

_____

_____

_____

_____

_____

Thank you.

_____
(Teacher's Name)

Grade or Class _____

School _____

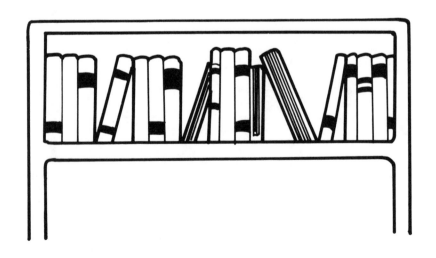

Letter 4–13: MEDICAL SERVICE REQUEST

TO: Classroom Teachers
FR: V. DiAngelo, Principal
RE: Medical Service Request

In order to ensure early medical attention for health problems among your pupils, you are asked to report below any known or suspected deviations from normal health, which in your opinion should have the attention of the school doctor or nurse. Include information you have received from parents or from the children themselves, as well as your own classroom observations.

Do not include simple vision problems and dental caries, which are separately reported. Do observe and report on:

- rate of growth
- posture and gait
- speech
- appearance and use of eyes
- hearing and ears
- condition of skin

- drowsiness or lethargy
- restlessness or irritability
- accidents
- unexplained drop in academic work
- excessive use of lavatory

Include any other items that seem significant, and put the record in the nurse's mailbox. The nurse will give these reports her immediate attention, and will confer with you on individual children as necessary.

Class _____ Room _____ Teacher _____

Child's Name   Health Problem

_____   _____

_____   _____

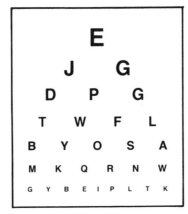

Letter 4–14: NEGATIVE REPLY TO APPLICANT

April 21, 19XX

Dear Ms. Ryder:

Thank you for your letter dated April 10. I regret sending a negative reply to someone who appears to be as qualified as you but we simply do not have an appropriate opening. At the moment we do not anticipate any positions in your field for next year. However, changes do occur unexpectedly from time to time. Please let me know as soon as possible if you are certified in some other area and whether or not you would consider an assignment in that area. We do anticipate openings in

_____.

Enclosed is an application blank and some literature about our district. Please complete the application, clearly indicating your second field of certification. It will probably be possible to shift you to the field of your first choice after a year or so should you accept employment in your second field. If your only interest is in your major field, I will keep your application in our active file and notify you immediately when an appropriate opening occurs.

Sincerely,

_____

V. DiAngelo, Principal

Letter 4-15: PARAPROFESSIONALS

TO: All Paraprofessionals and Teacher Assistants
RE: Checklist For Working In Early Childhood Classrooms
FR: V. DiAngelo, Principal

1. Do you enjoy working with very young children?

2. Do you sit down next to the child so that you are on his level and so that he may see your face and talk to you more easily?

3. Do you let the child do the talking while you listen attentively?

4. Are you alert to untied shoes, children who need a tissue, children who seem listless or ill?

5. Do you ask the teacher what to do about a child who is doing something of which you disapprove?

6. Do you speak clearly and slowly so that the child understands you?

7. Do you control your desire to talk constantly to the child?

8. Do you say "please" and "thank you" in talking with the children?

9. Do you give the child your full attention when he is speaking to you?

10. Do you use the correct names for things?

11. Do you print a child's name clearly on the back of his work?

12. Do you remind the children to wash their hands after painting or clay work?

13. Do you join in the playhouse activities by participating in the conversation, acting the role assigned to you by the children?

14. Do you sit with the children who are playing with table toys, listen to them, answer their questions?

15. Do you check at the end of the play period to see that no puzzle pieces are missing?

Letter 4–16: PUBLICATION

Dear Mrs. Hoogerhyde:

I was delighted to see your article "_____"
in the _____ issue of _____. It was a well
thought out and well-worded article. Your professional manner and school success are
now further enhanced by your having had an article published in a respected
journal/magazine.

We are all very proud of you at P.S. 54. May I photocopy your article and
provide each staff member with a copy? I would also like to send a copy to our
Superintendent and to each school board member. You are a credit to our school and to
your profession.

Sincerely,

_____

V. DiAngelo, Principal

Letter 4-17: REQUEST FOR INTERVIEW

Dear _____:

We would like to interview you for the position of _____.

There is a vacancy for which you are qualified in our _____.
We will conduct interviews in our administration building located at

_____. A map is enclosed to help you find it easily.

We are conducting interviews during the week of _____.
Please select a day and time convenient to you and indicate this on the enclosed addressed postcard. A visit while school is in session is most beneficial from the applicant's viewpoint.
We are looking forward to meeting you. Please bring your state certificate with you.

Sincerely,

_____

V. DiAngelo, Principal

Letter 4–18: REQUEST FOR MORE INFORMATION FROM APPLICANT

Dear Ms. Sanchez:

Thank you for your application form dated May 13. You omitted one or more of the items listed below. Please furnish the information checked below in the space provided here or, if necessary, on the reverse of this form. We will transfer it to your application form.

We lack only the item or items checked below:

Social Security number _____

Teacher Retirement number _____

Present address _____

Present phone number _____

Permanent address _____

Military status _____

Graduate work _____

_____

_____

References: (1) _____

(2) _____

(3) _____

Sincerely,

_____
V. DiAngelo, Principal

Letter 4–19: REQUEST FOR HEALTH SERVICE

Dear Hospital Administrator:

This year I am asking you again to provide a physical examination, including chest X-ray for each of our custodial and cafeteria workers. This will enable our food handlers to meet the Health Department requirements.

Please let me know what day of the week is most convenient for you as well as the time of day. We will need to have eight people examined.

Sincerely,

_____

V. DiAngelo, Principal

Letter 4–20: RETIREMENT

Dear Mr. Higgins:

    All of us at P.S. 54 wish you well on the occasion of your retirement after 30 years of service. We consider ourselves fortunate to have had a custodian of your caliber on our staff.

    We will miss seeing you each day and wish you the happy healthful retirement that you so richly deserve. Please keep in touch with us.

            Sincerely,

            _____

            V. DiAngelo, Principal

Letter 4–21: SAFETY PLAN

TO: All Staff Members
RE: School Safety Plan
FR: V. DiAngelo, Principal

After meeting with teachers, the Union chapter chairman, the custodian, and representatives of the PTA, the following school security plan has been formulated:

School Plant

1. The custodian will lock all doors from the outside, except the main entrance, every morning at 9:15 A.M. This will still permit the doors to be opened from the inside. Signs directing visitors to the General Office will be provided.

2. Visitors will be asked to sign a visitors' book stating their name, destination, and time of entrance and exit. Teachers will ask each visitor for a pass. They will ask any visitor who has no pass to obtain one in the General Office or at the lobby desk.

3. School aides or parent volunteers will staff this desk, located just inside the main entrance. Both the intercom and an outside telephone line will be available for their use.

4. The supervisory and custodial staff will periodically check doors to see that they are closed and in a locked position.

5. Teachers have been asked not to be in the building before 8:00 A.M. or after 4:30 P.M. except when an after-school activity is taking place.

6. The school public address system will be checked daily.

7. Mr. Barclay, vice principal, is the authorized representative in charge of safety when the principal is absent. Teacher alternates' names are posted in the General Office.

8. Upon suspicion that an intruder is in the building, a coded message will be broadcast: "Miss Smith, report to the Auditorium." This will alert teachers to lock their doors. The last word of the message will indicate where the principal or his delegate can be found for further instructions.

9. When classes are in session, pupils will use only Staircase 2 to go on errands. This will give us only one staircase to supervise throughout the day.

10. Unfamiliar visitors will be announced in the General Office by intercom telephone.

11. School property (A-V, athletic, music) will be marked with the school name, using an electric stylus or indelible ink.

12. First-aid kits will be checked weekly by the nurse. Fire extinguishers will be checked monthly by the custodian.

Staff

1. All teachers are aware of the school safety plan as well as of the emergency fire drill signals and procedures.
2. Teachers will keep all bulletins concerning emergency drills together in a folder available for reference and for a substitute to follow.
3. Periodically, teachers will review with their pupils basic safety measures and emergency signals and procedures.
4. Teachers will report any intruder to the office.
5. The principal will remove the intruder from the school building. Police will be called if necessary.
6. The lunch and custodial staff have been informed of our safety procedures.
7. Whistles are available for teachers who request them.

Pupils

1. All children are instructed in procedures for safety and emergency drill signals by their teachers.
2. Children must return to their classrooms when signals are sounded.
3. Pupils are instructed as to which entrances and exits they are to use during morning, lunch, and afternoon hours.
4. Pupils are instructed by their teachers to avoid contact with strangers that they may encounter near the school.

Parents and Community

1. Parents are asked to have their children arrive in school at or after 8:30 A.M. There is no supervision available before that hour.
2. Parents have provided the school with basic data; a Home Contact card including their telephone number at work, a neighbor's telephone number, and their physician's name and telephone number.
3. Community safety and health personnel (police, fire, hospital) have been consulted in formulating school safety plans.
4. Building inspections are made periodically by the Fire Department and Building Department teams.
5. The P.T.A. executive board was involved in formulating the safety plan and preparing the Home Contact Card.

Bomb Scare Procedures

- Upon receipt of a bomb threat, by telephone or otherwise, the recipient should immediately notify the head of the school. The information will then, without delay, be forwarded to the Police emergency operator—911.
- Particular emphasis should be placed on retaining the exact wording of the original message, and, if verbal, whether it was a male or female voice.

Demonstrations and Disorders

- All entrances to the building will be locked in the event of such an occurrence.
- All outside physical education classes will be cancelled.
- Teachers will remain with their classes and await instructions.
- If necessary, the police will be called.

Letter 4–22: SECRETARIES

TO: School Secretaries
RE: Procedures
FR: V. DiAngelo, Principal

1. Priorities

    a. First Aid for sick or injured pupil.
    b. Telephone calls—answer promptly.
    c. Report suspicious visitors.
    d. Safeguard confidential materials.
    e. Follow school procedures for bomb scares and emergencies.

2. Telephone etiquette

    a. Avoid long conversations.
    b. Give information clearly and succinctly.
    c. Screen calls politely. Determine reason for call and best person to answer it.
    d. Be aware of school activities that will affect your answers (trips, special events, teacher absence).
    e. Do not get involved in advice-giving or arguments. Refer caller to supervisor or counselor.

3. Visitor policies

    a. Acknowledge visitors promptly.
    b. Respond to questions politely.
    c. Direct visitor to appropriate staff member.
    d. Listen patiently to visitor who is unfamiliar with school procedures.
    e. Follow school rules relating to class visitation.
    f. If visitor is moving the child from the school building, ascertain the adult's relationship to the child.

Letter 4–23: SECURITY GUARDS

TO: School Security Guard
RE: Job Description
FR: V. DiAngelo, Principal

The following are the basic duties at P.S. 54. Other aspects of the job may evolve as you acquire additional experience.

1. The primary function of the guard is to screen visitors coming into the building. The guard must be at the lobby table at all times unless performing a related duty.

2. All outside doors must be locked. The guard will check these periodically.

3. The security of the building includes the play yard. Unauthorized persons are not to use the yard during school hours. It is the guard's responsibility to keep these people out of the yard.

4. At no time should the guard be in the lunchroom. If you feel certain that the doors are secure, the yard is free of trespassers, and the halls free of wanderers, then you should sit in the playroom outside the Boys' Room. Here you can check the safety of pupils at the drinking fountain as well as Exit 4 and the Boy's Room.

5. There must never be an occasion when someone enters the building without being questioned at the lobby table. During lunchtime the guard may be at the table or on duty in the gym, playroom, or yard.

6. Hours for guards are 8:40 A.M.–3:00 P.M. with 45 minutes for lunch. A school aide will cover the door during your lunch break. On the last school day of each month the security guard will give the secretary the sign-in sheets for that month. These will be filed. Be sure that the month and year appears on each sheet.

Letter 4–24: SUBSTITUTE TEACHER

TO: Substitute Teacher
RE: Feedback
FR: V. DiAngelo, Principal

Substitute Teacher _____ Class _____

Absent Teacher _____ Date _____

    1. I (used) (did not use) your lesson plans.
    2. I covered the following work:

       Reading _____

       Math _____

       Language Arts _____

       Other Areas _____

    3. Pupils Absent _____ Late _____
    4. Behavior Problems: (Name and incident)

    _____

    _____

    5. Comments:

    _____

    _____

    _____

    _____

                              _____
                              Signature of Substitute Teacher

Letter 4–25: SUBSTITUTE TEACHER

TO: Substitute Teacher
RE: Information Sheet
FR: V. DiAngelo, Principal

Welcome to P.S. 54. You are covering Class _____ today _____,

19_____. The regular teacher is _____.

Your buddy teacher is _____ in room _____. You will

meet your class at _____ in _____.

Fill in the attendance data in pencil. A folder "Instructions for Substitute" is in the top draw of the desk.

Special events for your class today include: _____

_____

In case of fire drill, follow class _____.

Special teacher duties are _____

Be sure to fill out Substitute Feedback Sheet and leave with the school secretary.

In case of an extended absence are you available tomorrow? _____

Comments of Substitute: _____

_____

_____

_____

_____

_____

Letter 4–26: SUSPENSION

TO: Selected Staff Members
RE: Suspension Hearing Summary
FR: V. DiAngelo, Principal

Name of pupil _____

Address _____

Date of birth _____   Telephone _____

Class _____   Teacher _____

Date pupil entered school _____

Date of pre-suspension letter sent _____

Date of pre-suspension conference _____

Date of principal's suspension conference _____

Date of return to school _____

    1. Current attendance for this school year:

       Present _____ Absent _____ Late _____ Cuts _____

    2. Agency, if any, to which pupil is known: _____

    3. Name of worker on case: _____

    4. Result of Agency contact: _____

    5. Persons present at conference: _____

       _____

    6. Reason(s) (specific) for suspension: _____

       _____

    7. Efforts of school personnel prior to suspension: _____

       _____

    8. Action(s) to be taken as a result of hearing:

       By school personnel _____

       By pupil _____

       By parent(s) of pupil _____

    9. Any other comments:

Letter 4-27: TEACHER–NURSE CONFERENCE

TO: School Nurse
RE: Teacher-Nurse Conference
FR: V. DiAngelo, Principal

Our conference is on _____ at _____ A.M./P.M. Before the conference:

1. Read the District Office bulletin on health conferences.
2. Plan ways to keep your class busy for about 30 minutes.
3. Make certain that there is a health card for every pupil.
4. Check to see that you have entered the height and weight.
5. Have scholastic records and roll book available for reference.
6. Review cards to discuss the following items.

During the conference we will discuss:

1. Children without important immunizations.
2. Unusual symptoms.
3. Emotional problems.
4. Frequent absences for the same reason or a variety of reasons.
5. Complaints of aches and pains.
6. Unusual hearing or vision problems.
7. Family health problems that may affect your pupils.
8. Other symptoms or signs you have noticed in your daily contact with your pupils.

After the conference:

1. Make a notation that a conference was held.
2. Refer pupils or parents to a clinic if that is the recommendation.

Letter 4–28: VENDOR COMPLAINT

Gentlemen:

We have received the following items from your company that do not meet the mandated specifications:

_____

_____

The contract specifically called for:

_____

_____

_____

Please contact us regarding this matter. Refer to Order # _____ dated _____.

Yours truly,

_____

V. DiAngelo, Principal

Letter 4–29: WARNING LIGHT

TO: Traffic Department

     I am writing to apprise you of a serious problem regarding morning traffic at P.S. 54. There have been several "close calls" at the intersection of Beekman Avenue and Grand View Street during these past two weeks.

     The stop sign was removed during the summer and cars go by without stopping. Many of our youngsters are being placed at risk without a blinking or warning light at that corner. There is real danger without a warning light.

     Please take steps to install warning lights around our school. We do not want to place our children in a dangerous situation.

Sincerely,

_____

V. DiAngelo, Principal

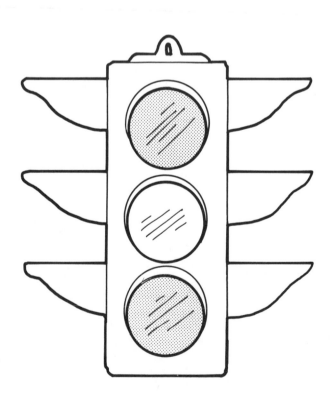

SECTION
5

Letters
for
Special Events

Letter 5–1: AMERICAN HERITAGE CONTEST

TO: Pupils and Parents
RE: American Heritage Contest
FR: V. DiAngelo, Principal

Our country prides itself on the rich and varied backgrounds of its citizens. Many different racial, religious, and national groups have contributed to our American heritage.

We are going to hold a poster contest commemorating the pride we have in our American heritage. The theme will vary with each contestant. Some ideas for a title include:

America—One Out of Many
Sweet Land of Liberty
They Built Our Land
Old World—New Dreams
A Nation of Immigrants

The artwork should be done on oak tag or poster board no larger than 18″ by 24″. Any art media may be used: crayon, water color, pastels, pen and ink, markers.

Be sure your name, class, and address appear on the back. Entries must be

brought to school by _____.

Prizes include a $50 Government Bond. Selected entries will be displayed around the school before being returned.

All pupils who enter will receive a Commendation Card.

Letter 5–2: ART CONTEST

TO: Pupils in Grades 4–6
FR: V. DiAngelo, Principal
RE: Art Contest

      We are going to have a Pupil Art Show along the schoolyard fence in May. Feel free to submit original art work on any subject or theme. Please observe the guidelines mentioned below.

GUIDELINES

Eligibility:	Pupils in Grades 4 through 6, including Special Education.
Number of Entries:	Each class may submit up to five entries.
Due Date:	Deliver art work to the office by _____.
Identification:	Each entry must have an 8″ × 5″ card pasted to its reverse side which includes the pupil's name, class, and home address.
Medium:	Any medium such as pen and ink drawing, painting, printmaking, collage, montage, cut paper, or a combination of any of the above.
Materials:	Any appropriate materials such as tempera or poster paint, markers, drawing inks, pastels, water colors, cut paper, etc.
Dimensions:	No larger than 14″ × 18″ unmatted or unmounted.
Judging Criteria:	Work will be judged for the pupil's
	(a) Imaginative use of materials and media
	(b) Unique interpretation of the theme
	(c) Creativity in ability to use art media
Prizes:	To be announced

Letter 5-3: BUS SAFETY CONTEST

TO: All Pupils
RE: School Bus Safety Contest
FR: V. DiAngelo, Principal

   Your safety on the bus is very important to all of us. We are going to hold a poster contest with the theme "Us on the Bus." Each class may select two posters. A committee of teachers, parents, and pupils will select from that number two posters to represent our school in the statewide competition.
   Poster themes must be original and must stress safety. Designs should be on good oak tag or heavy paper. At least part of a yellow school bus must appear in the poster.
   Freehand drawn letters only may be used on the poster design. Stenciled, preprinted or press-on letters may not be used.
   Any type of medium such as print, crayon, cut paper, felt pen, etc. may be used on the poster. Posters will be judged on their visual impact and originality.
   Be sure to include your name, grade, age, school, and teacher's name on the back of your poster design. All state entries become the property of the National School Bus Safety Week Committee.
   Good luck!

Letter 5–4: CAREER DAY

April 3, 19XX

Dear Ms. Bulloch:

I am seeking your help. We at P.S. 54 are planning a "Career Day" to be held on May 1. At that time we are going to have speakers from various fields stationed in different classrooms. After a brief welcome in the Auditorium our pupils will go to those classrooms where a representative of their field of interest will greet them. It is suggested that each guest speaker make a presentation of about ten minutes and then take questions.

We recognize you as a role model for our pupils in the field of engineering. It would be our pleasure to present you to our pupils as a resource person. Please let us know if you can join us on May 1 at 10 o'clock.

We have found in the past that our pupils want to know the requirements for the career, what they may expect in a typical day, and some personal anecdotes.

After the last session, at approximately 12 o'clock, the P.T.A. will have refreshments for all the participants. I have also requested that a photographer be present.

Please call me at 761-5511. I do hope you will say "yes" when you call.

Sincerely,

_____

V. DiAngelo, Principal

Letter 5–5: CLEANUP CONTEST

TO: All Pupils
FR: V. DiAngelo, Principal
RE: "Team Up to Clean Up" Contest

Our school will hold a contest to see which class can earn the most points in a cleanup campaign. We are calling it: Team Up to Cleanup.

With your teacher, look around the school community for an area that needs cleaning up. It could be in our building, around the outside of the school, a vacant lot, or some other area in our school neighborhood that needs cleaning up.

Describe your project on one sheet of paper: the problem area, e.g. classroom, lunchroom, schoolyard, block, park, etc. Take "before and after" pictures. Get written statements from adults who know the area well.

Points will be awarded based on the size of the problem, the degree of success, and the age of the pupils.

The winning class will have its picture in the local newspaper, a pizza party, and prizes for each pupil participating.

Good luck!

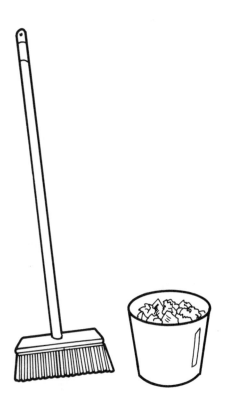

Letter 5–6:   EARTH DAY

Dear Teachers and Neighbors of P.S. 54:

Soon we will welcome the first day of spring. On March 20 at 1:13 P.M. (Eastern Standard Time), the moment at which the vernal equinox occurs, or the spring season begins astronomically, we will also celebrate EARTH DAY.

In preparation for Earth Day you should begin now to plan events to precede, take place on, and follow the March 20th date. As a guide, I have prepared the following list of suggested activities:

1. Prepare graphic displays on environmental problems, energy needs, food needs, housing, land use, recycling, and waters around us.

2. Survey and record the sources that contribute to the pollution of the school neighborhood.

3. Survey and record the sources that contribute to pollution in the homes. Map out and take steps to eliminate these sources.

4. Present assembly programs to demonstrate the science of measuring and checking pollution.

5. Post reports of pollution levels on bulletin boards.

6. Prepare exhibits on the effects of pollution on living things.

7. Have classes write and present plays related to one or more aspects of Earth Day.

8. Distribute seeds and seedlings for pupils to plant and care for.

9. Plant trees as symbols of renewal.

10. Organize pupils into Volunteer Air Pollution Observator and Reporter (VAPOR) squads to keep track of and work to eliminate neighborhood sources of pollution.

11. Set up antilitter squads to campaign for cleaner streets.

12. Publish an antipollution bulletin. Give specific steps that parents and pupils can take to reduce pollution at home, at school, and in the neighborhood.

13. Arrange visits to environmental centers, museums, parks, wildlife sanctuaries and zoos.

14. Draw posters or write compositions on such themes as:
    The Wonder of Life
    Pollution—Spoiler of Life
    What I Can Do to Stop Pollution

Earth Day (Ecology Day) provides us with an unusual opportunity to raise the level of pupil awareness and understanding of the fact that people, and only people, can guarantee that Planet Earth will remain hospitable for generations to come.

V. DiAngelo, Principal

Letter 5–7: ETHNIC FAIR

TO: All Parents
RE: Ethnic Fair
FR: V. DiAngelo, Principal

Our nation was built by people of different ethnic groups. In an effort to foster

understanding of the contributions made by _____-Americans, our school will

hold _____-American Week from _____ to _____.
Each grade will celebrate according to its level of understanding and class
schedule. Your child's teacher will send you an invitation.

We invite you to help us spread an appreciation of _____-American
Heritage by helping your child's teacher to:

_____ prepare a national food item.

_____ teach a folk dance.

_____ display traditional costumes.

_____ obtain a copy of a current newspaper or magazine from

_____.

_____ put up a bulletin board display of travel posters and maps.

Your assistance will be greatly appreciated as would any ideas you have
in furthering an increased understanding of the unique contributions of the

_____.

Letter 5–8: FAMILY LIVING MEETING

TO: All Parents
FR: V. DiAngelo, Principal
RE: Family Living Meeting

You are invited to attend a series of workshops dealing with children/family relationships and sexuality.

DATES: Wednesdays, March 10, 17, 24, and 31
TIMES: 9:30 A.M.—coffee
        9:30–11:30 A.M.—workshop for district parents
PLACE: P.S.54 Auditorium

The topics to be discussed include:

- Puberty-Physical Development
- Dealing with Peers
- Marriage
- Single Parents
- Dealing with Death, Siblings, and Divorce
- Sexual Development
- Family Planning
- Communication Skills (Improving Communications with Children)
- Open Suggested Topics of Personal Concern

For additional information, call the Guidance Office at 761-5924. Admission is FREE and door prizes will be given out at each workshop.

I hope to see you at the workshops!

Letter 5–9: FIELD DAY

TO: School Neighbors
RE: Field Day

    We are inviting all our friends who live near our school to participate in next month's Field Day. This list of events will enhance your enjoyment. We are also looking for some volunteer judges.

1. Relay Race: The two teams may have boys and girls or may have both boys and girls on the same team.

2. Dash: Ten students at a time will run. First, second, and third place winners will run in the semifinals.
   a. Preliminaries: There will be approximately 120 students in 12 races; there will be 36 winners.
   b. Semifinals: There will be 36 students in 4 races; there will be 12 winners.
   c. Finals: There will be 12 students, 6 racing at a time, with the top 2 in each race running in the championships.

3. Softball Throw: The top 10 from each grade will compete.

4. Bean Bag Toss: There will be a group of boxes, each having a different point value. The contestant will get three tosses and those with the most points will win.

5. Distance Run: There will be one complete run around the school; 10 contestants running at the same time.

6. Ping-Pong Ball Throw: The students will see who can throw the ball the greatest distance. This will take place in the gym.

7. Thirty-second Basketball: The students will see how many foul shots they can make in 30 seconds. This will take place in the gym.

8. Frisbee Throw for Accuracy: The students must throw accurately along a center line. The distance they throw is subtracted from the line.

Remember the date: Tuesday, May 11, 19XX.
Please come to the school at 9 o'clock. Judges should report 30 minutes earlier.

       Thank you!

       ————————————————
       V. DiAngelo, Principal

Letter 5–10: FINAL ASSEMBLY

May 24, 19XX

Dear Parents of Seventh Grade Pupils:

We are pleased to invite you to our Seventh Grade Final Assembly on Friday morning, June 11, 19XX at 9:30 A.M. in our school auditorium.

This is a joyous occasion for our pupils, and a proud one for our teachers who have nurtured these young people through the grades. For this special assembly, we are asking that pupils follow this simple dress code:

Boys: Shirt, tie, no jacket
Girls: <u>Simple</u> summer dress or skirt and blouse; no halters, no shorts, no clogs

Our guest speaker will be Carl Greenberg, the School Board Chairperson.

At the conclusion of the Final Assembly, at approximately 11:00 A.M., pupils and guests will be excused for an extended lunch hour.

Congratulations and best wishes!

Sincerely,

_____

V. DiAngelo, Principal

Reminder to Pupils: Attendance at this Assembly is a privilege. Pupils who misbehave will NOT be allowed to attend.

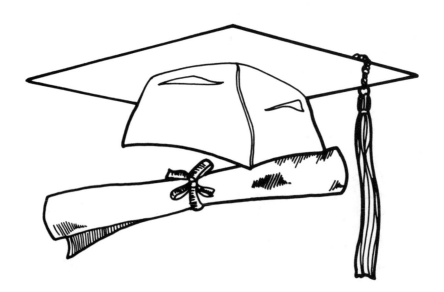

Letter 5–11: FOREIGN LANGUAGE WEEK

TO: Parents of Pupils Studying a Foreign Language
FR: V. DiAngelo, Principal
RE: Foreign Language Week

    We are proud of those boys and girls at our school who are studying a foreign language. The week of January 14 has been designated as Foreign Language Week at P.S. 54. We will mark this occasion by fostering a wider study of foreign languages and displaying the competence of our foreign language students.
    During Foreign Language Week the following activities have been planned by our teachers. Your child's teacher will send home an invitation giving time and place,

written by pupils in English and _____.

1. Food Fair featuring _____ foods.
2. Assembly Program including songs and dances.
3. Bulletin Board display of everyday expressions and pictures.
4. Booklet of pen pal letters from around the world.
5. Videotape of bilingual skits featuring our pupils acting, with English subtitles.

We hope you will be able to attend.

Letter 5–12: GRANDPARENTS DAY

TO: All Parents and Grandparents

Salute to Grandparents

Date: Friday, October 17, 19XX
Time: 1:30 P.M.

Grandparents play a large role in the lives of our pupils. In recent years, in many families, grandparents have taken on an even greater role because of single-parent families and working mothers. In all cases, grandparents have provided additional warmth, care, and concern—three important nutrients that help growing children thrive.

We at P.S. 54 want to salute the grandparents of our pupils with a big "thank you." Ours will be a musical salute in the Auditorium on Friday, October 17 at 1:30 P.M.

Our musical program will feature third, fourth, and fifth graders:

Class 3–"America, We Love You"
Class 4–"Frolicking Tonetteers"
Grade 5 Band–"Golden Days of Music"

This is a special invitation for _all_ grandparents to attend. While grandparents will get the best seats, we will admit parents who hope to be grandparents someday.

V. DiAngelo, Principal

Letter 5–13: MATH BEE

TO: Classroom Teachers
FR: V. DiAngelo, Principal
RE: School Math Bee

On Tuesday, December 6, 19XX at 9:30 A.M., we will hold a Math Bee in the Auditorium. The purpose of this competition is to stimulate pupil facility with number facts and mental arithmetic.

Please prepare your pupils by holding a Class Math Bee in your classroom in the next two weeks. Use flash cards with mental math problems appropriate to your grade level. Send the names of the two top math winners to the office.

At the school wide competition, we will team up the class winners. Prizes will be awarded to all who enter. The P.T.A. is providing a Saving Bond to the schoolwide winner.

Remember, no written computations or calculators may be used. A two-minute timer will be used for each contestant.

Good luck!

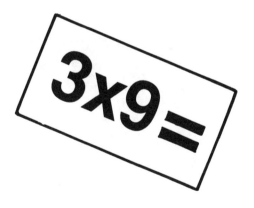

Letter 5–14: PAN AMERICAN HERITAGE

TO: Pan American Union Bilingual Teachers
FR: V. DiAngelo, Principal
RE: Pan American Heritage and Culture Week

Our school will celebrate the contributions of Pan Americans to our country. We will celebrate the week of April _____.

The school library has a display of books on Pan America. Our librarian, Ms. Tindell, has prepared an impressive bibliography.

This bibliography may be used to teach Pan American History and Culture. It includes listings of appropriate books, records, cassettes, films, and visual materials. Information may be found on various countries such as: Argentina, Brazil, Cuba, Mexico, Dominican Republic, Ecuador, Haiti, Costa Rica, Panama, and Venezuela. This publication will be made available to all upon request.

A poster commemorating Pan American Heritage and Culture Week for our school has been designed and produced by Class 6B.

I invite your suggestions for making this event a success.

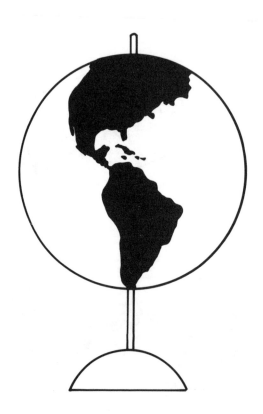

Letter 5–15: PHYSICAL FITNESS AWARDS

TO: All Pupils in Grades 4, 5, 6, and 7
RE: Physical Fitness Awards Program
FR: V. DiAngelo, Principal

Our school is going to hold a Youth Fitness Test. It will be held as a regular part of our physical education program in grades four through seven.

Youngsters who achieve between 50 percent and 80 percent on this test will receive a Physical Fitness Achievement Certificate. A special award button will be given to those pupils who achieve in the top 20 percent.

Your teacher has a score chart for each grade. The test items include:

Boys	Girls
Situps (flexed Leg)	Situps (flexed leg)
Pull ups	Flexed Arm Hang
Standing Long Jump	Standing Long Jump
50-Yard Dash	50-Yard Dash
600-Yard Run	600-Yard Run
Shuttle Run	Shuttle Run

I urge everyone to participate. Samples of last year's certificates and award buttons are on display in the Gym.

Letter 5–16: PUMPKIN DECORATING CONTEST

October 12, 19XX

Dear Parents:

We invite your child to participate in our annual Pumpkin Decorating Contest. In an effort to foster creativity and enhance our pupils' excitement concerning Halloween, we will hold this contest in school on Tuesday, October 28. Pumpkins will be displayed in the lunchroom with each pupil's name and class on a label.

Essentially, pupils may:

1. Decorate a pumpkin at home.
2. Bring it to school on Tuesday, October 28, 19XX.
3. Display pumpkins in the lunchroom that morning, with a name and class label.

Classes will be invited to view the display. Pumpkins will be taken home Tuesday afternoon. Small children with small arms should bring small pumpkins.

While participation will be voluntary, this is a great opportunity for pupils to work on a safe, wholesome Halloween project at home that he or she can share in a positive way with his or her schoolmates.

Pumpkins will not be judged, nor will there be prizes. Every child who brings a decorated pumpkin will receive a Commendation Card. No candles may be used. Please identify the pumpkin with name and class on a visible tag.

Encourage your child to participate! Parents may view pumpkins in the lunchroom between 9:00 A.M. and 10:45 A.M. At 10:45 A.M. all pumpkins must be removed as we prepare for Kindergarten Lunch.

Sincerely,

_____

V. DiAngelo, Principal

Letter 5-17: PUPIL-OF-THE-MONTH AWARD

TO: All Staff Members
FR: V. DiAngelo, Principal
RE: Pupil-of-the-Month Award

We have so many fine students at P.S. 54. In order to call attention to those pupils who distinguish themselves in some positive way we have put up a "Pupil of the Month" bulletin board outside the school office.

Each staff member (teacher, aide, lunchroom, or custodial staff) is invited to send a short note to the principal citing a pupil for some good deed or special commendation. We have an instamatic camera and will photograph the "Pupil of the Month." His or her picture will appear next to a 3″ × 5″ typed card along with name, class, and a brief description of the good deed.

Some suggestions for recommending a pupil may include the following, but are surely not limited to:

1. Winner of a contest or community event
2. "Most improved" pupil
3. Finder of wallet returned intact
4. High achievement
5. School or community service

Please take a close look at your students with an eye toward recommending a "Pupil of the Month."

Pupil-of-the-Month Nomination

Name _____ Class _____ Date __

Reason _____

_____

_____

_____

_____

Pupil of the Month

Letter 5–18: SCIENCE FAIR

TO: PARENTS
RE: SCHOOL SCIENCE FAIR SUGGESTIONS

Our school science fair will not be held until after the first of the year. However, it is not too early for your youngster to start thinking about his or her science project. You may wish to use this opportunity to plan together, but let the child do the work. The following suggestions will help you reduce the tension and increase the fun and learning:

Exhibits should follow scientific procedure. For example, each should have a control or comparison to help provide proof that certain procedures, additions, or deletions, produce different results. An example of this would be two plants, one without water, or heat, or light, and the other with. Without some comparison there is no scientific exhibit.

Social Studies dioramas, pictures or charts, rock or other small collections are nice but have little scientific impact unless a point is proven. Pupils should be encouraged to devise a scientific experiment in using these materials.

Please do not submit an exhibit that shows direct parental involvement, including the printing.

Pupils should have signs that readily explain the exhibit but they must be able to talk about it and show that they know a great deal about the science facts involved, on their grade level.

Commercial kits are not advised. An extensive background is needed to explain the kit well enough.

No live animals should be exhibited.

No electricity or matches should be used by students in grades K to 6. Special permission is needed for seventh grade students.

The following titles, collected from recent winners at the Borough Science Fair, will give you additional ideas:

Earthworms at Work	Growth of Molds
The Best Insulation	Seeing Is Not Always Believing
A Waterlens Microscope	Magnets—Properties and Use
How Heat Affects Materials	Making New Paper from Old
How Nutrients Affect Plant Growth	Water Absorption by Soil
Pinhole Photography	Producing Sound by Strings
Growing Crystals	Solar Energy
A Model Water Filter	

Remember, this is a voluntary activity. If it becomes a tension-producing experience, drop it and try again a week later. We would like to see every child submit an entry.

Letter 5–19:   SCIENCE FAIR

TO: Teachers
FR: V. DiAngelo, Principal
RE: School Science Fair

This year the Science Fair will be held on Thursday, January 24.

Grades 2 through 7 will participate in the School Fair.

Kindergarten and First Grade may hold Class Science Fairs if they wish; they will not exhibit with the other grades.

The two Seventh Grade winners will represent P.S. 54 in the County Science Fair which will be held at Madison High School on Friday, March 18, 19XX (judging) and Saturday, March 19, 19XX (Public Viewing).

- There may be individual or group projects.
- There may be no more than <u>three</u> children in a group.
- Class projects are <u>not</u> accepted.
- The project must be made by the <u>pupil</u>. Adult assistance (parent or teacher) should be in the form of suggestions <u>only</u>.
- The project must be on a topic applicable to the pupil's grade. (See the Science Manual for your grade.)
- The project should be three-dimensional, with labels and/or an accompanying diagram. The pupil must be able to explain his/her project and to answer questions on it.
- Avoid the use of glass or any materials that could be dangerous. Matches, if needed, should be handled by a teacher. No vertebrates are to be exhibited.

The class teacher will select the three best projects for exhibition in the school fair.

Send to the Office on Monday, January 21, on a 3 × 5 card, the name and class of each pupil selected as a class science fair winner. You will receive the schedule of class visits to the Science Fair next week.

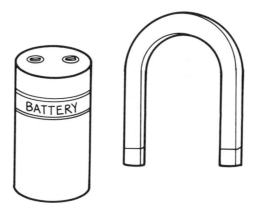

Letter 5–20: SCIENCE FAIR

TO: Homeroom Teachers
FR: V. DiAngelo, Principal
RE: Science Fair

The P.S. 54 School Science Fair will be held on Monday, January 21, and Thursday, January 24, 19XX, according to the following schedule:

Monday, January 21–Grades 1 and 2 (Auditorium)
       Grade 3   (Room 318)

Thursday, January 24–Grade 4 and 5 (A.M.) (Room 318)
        Grade 6 and 7 (P.M.) (Room 318)

A panel of judges will visit the classrooms of Grades 1, 2, and 3 on Thursday, January 17, and Grades 4–7 on Friday, January 19, to select the projects that will be on display.

Procedures

1. Projects must be on or above grade level.
2. Each pupil must be able to answer questions to show that he/she has a thorough working knowledge of the project.
3. Teachers and/or judges may disqualify any project that in their judgment reflects parental involvement.
4. Participation is optional.

The schedule for setup times and class visitations will be distributed at a later date.

Please direct any questions concerning the Fair to Mr. Mistretta.

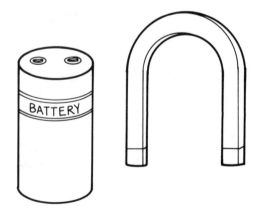

Letter 5–21: SEX EDUCATION EVALUATION

TO: Participants
RE: Sex Education Seminar Evaluation Sheet

1. The single most helpful part of the seminar series was _____

   _____

   _____

2. The least useful part for me was _____

   _____

   _____

3. I was most deeply touched by _____

   _____

   _____

4. I was most angry or irritated when _____

   _____

   _____

5. The main new things I learned were _____

   _____

   _____

6. My thinking changed most with regard to _____

   _____

   _____

7. I feel I need to know more about _____

   _____

   _____

8. As a group, I feel we were _____ were not _____ able to establish mutually helpful contacts and relationships with each other that can go beyond the conclusions of these seminars. I think this is primarily due to _____

_____

_____

9. I think other parents should _____ should not _____ sign up for these seminars because _____

_____

_____

10. As a direct result of my participation in these seminars, I plan to _____

_____

_____

11. If you were to plan similar seminars, I suggest that you _____

_____

_____

12. I'd just like to add in closing _____

_____

_____

Please return this evaluation sheet to the seminar leader.

_____

Signature (Optional)

Letter 5–22: SOCIAL STUDIES OLYMPIAD

TO: Social Studies Teachers
FR: V. DiAngelo, Principal
RE: Social Studies Olympiad

Welcome to the National Social Studies Olympiad to be held in our school during the week of March 18.

Enclosed please find:

1. Three (3) copies of each Contest (including answer sheet) that you have entered. You may reproduce as many copies as you need.

2. One (1) copy of the answer key for each Contest you have entered.

3. One (1) score sheet for each Contest you have entered.

4. One (1) return-addressed envelope so that you may return to us the top copy of the score sheet. The yellow copy is for your records.

5. One medal for each participating team.

6. Ten (10) certificates for each participating team. On each certificate there is a space for designating the Contest and the year. Please fill in the name of the appropriate Contest; i.e. ELEMENTARY—GRADE 5.

In the event that students are tied for any of the awards, we suggest that you propose a question to them that will serve as a "tie-breaker."

CONTEST REGULATIONS

1. It is expected that each teacher will preserve the integrity of the Contest by adhering to the appropriate time limitation (35 minutes) and by maintaining adequate security of the materials prior to the Contest.

2. Teachers are not permitted to assist students in any way.

3. If, for any reason, you wish to appeal an answer, please write a brief description of your appeal on the back of the score sheet.

SCORING

1. Score the papers using the answer key provided. Accept an answer as correct only if it is the same as the answer in the answer key.

2. On the score sheet, list the names of the top ten (10) scorers for the Contest. Their total is your team score for the Contest.

Thank you for your cooperation. We hope your students enjoy the Contest.

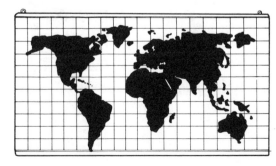

Letter 5–23: SPECIAL EVENTS—SEPTEMBER

TO: All Teachers
RE: September Special Events

The return to school provides us with some special dates that will help add spark to your lessons.

September 10: Native American Day. Our library will have a display of books about American Indians. Emphasize their many contributions to our county. The library bulletin board will have names and locations of local tribes.

September 15: Birthday of Grandma Moses. Use this as a springboard for a discussion of the role of senior citizens. Display examples of primitive art. Use reproductions to study life in New England.

September 22: First Day of Autumn. Use this opportunity to show how rotations of the earth and its revolving around the sun affects day and night as well as seasons of the year.

Better Breakfast Month. This is a good opportunity to develop units on nutrition and health. Make a survey to see what your pupils eat for breakfast. Discuss the school breakfast program.

<u>Events with dates that vary each year:</u>

National Hispanic Heritage Week. Highlight the geographic closeness of Puerto Rico and the Caribbean Islands.

U.S. Constitution Week. Emphasize the need for all citizens to be concerned about their community.

Letter 5–24: SPECIAL EVENTS—OCTOBER

TO: All Teachers
RE: October Special Events

This first full month of school provides you with several enrichment activities for your class.

Columbus Day: Have pupils trace the routes of Columbus and other explorers. Discuss the claims of Leif Ericson as the first European to land in the New World.

William Penn's Birthday: Discuss the life of this Quaker and the quest for religious freedom.

United Nations Week: Focus on the concept of world citizenship. Point out ways in which all the world's citizens are alike.

Fire Prevention Week: Remind pupils that fire drills are important at home as well as in school.

End of Daylight Savings Time: Help pupils understand that D.S.T. ends at 2 A.M. on the last Sunday of this month and Standard Time resumes. "What does the sun have to do with the length of daylight?"

Letter 5–25: SPECIAL EVENTS—NOVEMBER

TO: All Teachers
RE: November Special Events

This month offers several opportunities to stimulate your pupils.

<u>November 1</u>: Author's Day. This has been celebrated since 1928 on this date. Help pupils understand the creative process. Discuss some of their favorite authors.

<u>First Tuesday</u>: Election Day. Help pupils understand the current races in your community. Make posters urging adults to vote.

<u>November 11</u>: Veteran's Day. Have pupils discuss the concepts of war and peace, on their grade level. Ask a veteran's group for information about an essay contest.

<u>November 19</u>: Gettysburg Address. On this day President Lincoln delivered his famous speech.

<u>Fourth Thursday</u>: Thanksgiving Day. Have pupils draw pictures of those things for which they are most grateful.

Letter 5–26: SPECIAL EVENTS—DECEMBER

TO: All Teachers
RE: December Special Events

    December is a busy month, but these items are sure to perk up your lessons.

    December 5: Phillis Wheatley died in 1884. This black woman was a famous poet during the colonial period. Some of her poems are suitable for reading aloud on almost any grade level.

    December 6: St. Nicholas Day. Research this holiday as it is enjoyed in Belgium. Have your pupils contrast the appearance of St. Nicholas, Kris Kringle, Father Christmas, and, of course, Santa Claus.

    December 7: Pearl Harbor Day. Anniversary of Japan's surprise attack in 1941. Locate Pearl Harbor on a wall map. Discuss current relations with Japan.

    December 16: Boston Tea Party. In 1773 there was a raid on three British ships by American patriots. Discuss the importance of tea in colonial times.

    December 21: Pilgrims land at Plymouth Rock, 1620. Set up committees to study the contributions of immigrants to this country. Consider why each group left their homeland to come to this country. Start with the Pilgrims.

    December 25: Celebrated all over the world by Christians as the birthday of Jesus Christ. People take part in religious ceremonies. People exchange gifts and decorate their homes. This custom of exchanging gifts began in memory of the gifts that shepherds and the Wise Men brought to the Christ child. This is observed as a national as well as a religious holiday in most countries.

    Eight-day period, usually in December (consult Jewish calendar). Hanukkah, the Festival of Lights. The candles on the Hanukkah menorah will burn in many Jewish homes during this week. Show the McGraw-Hill filmstrip "Hanukkah," or ask the librarian for some Jewish holiday books.

Letter 5–27: SPECIAL EVENTS—JANUARY

TO: All Teachers
RE: January Special Events

Now that the holidays are over, we still have some special events to add sparkle to your lessons.

January 1: New Year's Day. Anticipate this day by asking children what they think "turning over a new leaf" means. Discuss New Year's resolutions.

January 6: Three Kings Day. This is an important holiday if you have Puerto Rican pupils. Epiphany. This is a Greek Orthodox, Christian, and Protestant holiday.

January 7: Russian Christmas. Check your current calendar. Feast of St. John the Baptist. This is observed by Greek Orthodox. Discuss different calendars.

January 11: Ashura. This is an Islamic fast day commemorating the death of the grandson of Mohammed.

January 13: Stephen Foster's Birthday. Discuss the old South as compared to the present South.

January 15:Martin Luther King Day. Help students learn more about this leader. What was his "dream"? Talk about nonviolence as a philosphy.

January 17: Benjamin Franklin's birthday. Have a class "Poor Richard Club" meeting like the one that convenes in Philadelphia every year on this day. Point out Franklin's many accomplishments.

Sometimes in January: Chinese New Year. Display some books about Chinese children, such as May May by Leo Politi (Scribner) and Chinese in America by Claire Jones (Lerner). Display some pictures of the Chinese New Year celebration, including the dancing animals.

Letter 5–28: SPECIAL EVENTS—FEBRUARY

TO: All Teachers
RE: February Special Events

The shortest month is not short of special events that you can share with your pupils.

February 1: National Freedom Day. This commemorates the day in 1865 when President Lincoln signed a bill outlawing slavery. Have pupils write about the freedoms they enjoy. Discuss the restrictions that all of us have on our freedoms. What responsibilities does freedom carry with it?

February 1–7: National Children's Dental Health Week. Ask a dental hygenist to talk to the pupils in class. Arrange with the local dental society to get samples and literature from toothpaste companies.

February 8–15: Black History Week. Consult "The Black Experience in Children's Books," compiled by Augusta Baker for the New York Public Library. This is a bibliography featuring a rich variety of materials.

February 12: Lincoln's Birthday. Select a sound filmstrip on the life of Lincoln. Emphasize the deep concern that President Lincoln had for saving the Union. How many of these problems still exist today?

February 14: St. Valentine's Day. Do some research into the background of this enjoyable day. You will find some interesting conjectures on the real St. Valentine. Relate your activities to a fund-raising project for the local Heart Fund. They will love you for it.

February 15: Susan B. Anthony Day. Read about the life of this famous American who was born on this day. If she were alive today what would be some of her concerns?

February 22: Washington's Birthday. Focus on Mount Vernon. What kind of life style did George Washington enjoy? What were some of his activities when home at Mount Vernon? Compare the architecture of this building to that of other well-known residences.

Letter 5–29: SPECIAL EVENTS—MARCH

TO: All Teachers
RE: March Special Events

Now that winter is behind us, your pupils will enjoy celebrating some of these special events.

March 5: Crispus Attucks Day. Explore the role of Black people in colonial times.

Second Week: Girl Scout Week. Discuss terms "Brownie," "Intermediate," and "Senior Scouts." Tell story of Juliette Low of Savannah, Georgia. Look up scouting in encyclopedia.

March 9: Amerigo Vespucci's Birthday. Recall events of other Italian navigators and explorers.

March 14: Prophet's Birthday. Islamic holiday. Use a wall map and trace the countries of the Middle East.

March 17: St. Patrick's Day. Prepare hall bulletin boards.

Fourth Week: National Poison Prevention Week. Prepare units in health education classes.

Usually in March: Jewish holiday of Purim—Story of Queen Esther. Annunciation of Virgin Mary—Greek Orthodox.

Letter 5–30: SPECIAL EVENTS—APRIL

TO: All Teachers
RE: April Special Events

In order to help your pupils keep their spirits high, use these April energizers.

First Week: National Library Week. Make sure that every pupil in your class has a library card. Plan a class trip to the library. Call ahead to see if you can show your class how books are accessioned and prepared for the shelves.

April 4: (varies with calendar) Han Shih Festival. Chinese holiday sometimes called Cold Food Feast. Point out that spaghetti and many other dishes had their origin in China.

April 5: Booker T. Washington's Birthday. Show a filmstrip illustrating the hardships this great American overcame.

Second Week: Pan American Week (April 14 is Pan American Day). Invite parents and other adults to attend a program depicting the many contributions made by North, Central, and South Americans to the quality of life in our hemisphere.

April 13: Thomas Jefferson's Birthday. Highlight this president's talent for invention.

April 17: Verrazano Day. This is an excellent opportunity to show role of Italian navigators in our country's development. Show picture of Verrazano Bridge in New York.

April 23: William Shakespeare's Birthday. Trace the development of English and American literature.

Passover: Jewish holiday that comes at different times in the spring. It commemorates the exodus of the Jews from Egypt.

Letter 5–31: SPECIAL EVENTS—MAY

TO: All Teachers
RE: May Special Events

There are many special events to commemorate this month with your class.

May 1: Loyalty Day. Discuss concepts of patriotism and loyalty to family, country, and ideals.

May 1: Lei Day in Hawaii. Garlands of flowers are worn in our 50th state on this day as a symbol of good will and friendliness.

The month of May is Radio Month. Make a class survey of the number of hours each week that each child listens to the radio. What kinds of programs are heard? What percentage of radio listening is to a car radio? A transistor?

Prepare for Mother's Day with a crafts project.

Second Week: Police Week. Emphasize the positive aspects of a policeman's or policewoman's job.

Third Week: National Transportation Week and World Trade Week. Mention both in a discussion of man's interdependence on others for raw and manufactured materials.

May 20: Amelia Earhart began her solo flight across the Atlantic Ocean on this date in 1932. This was the first such flight by a woman. Discuss the opportunities for women today that did not exist in 1932.

Last Monday in May: Memorial Day. Commemorate this occasion by planting a tree or shrub in the school garden in honor of our fallen heroes.

Letter 5-32: SPECIAL EVENTS—JUNE

TO: All Teachers
RE: June Special Events

    In this last month of the school year, besides having graduation and the summer recess on their minds, you can impress your pupils with the following:

    June 3: Jefferson Davis' Birthday. This is a legal holiday in Florida, Georgia, and Louisiana. It is observed on the first Monday in June in Alabama and Mississippi. Ask your pupils, "Who is this President and when did he rule?"

    June 11: King Kamehameha I Day. This is a public holiday in Hawaii. Ask your pupils, "Which of the 50 states was once ruled by Kings and Queens?" Use this as a springboard for a discussion of how Hawaii moved from monarchy to territory to state.

    June 14: Flag Day. Discuss the origin of the American flag. Ask pupils to draw replicas of our flag at different stages.

    June 17: Bunker Hill Day. Why is this celebrated in Massachusetts? Why is it important for all Americans?

    Father's Day: Third Sunday in June. How do you think this celebration began? What special qualities do you think a good father has? What do you think your father (or grandfather or uncle or stepfather) would like more than anything else on this day?

Letter 5–33: STORYTELLING CONTEST

Dear Parents:

Does your child like to tell stories? I don't mean falsehoods, but imaginative tales geared to entertain rather than deceive. People of all ages enjoy hearing and telling a good story.

Our school is going to have a Storytelling Contest for pupils in Grades 3, 4, 5, and 6. The school winners will participate in district and citywide competitions to be held in April. Younger pupils in our school will be able to hear the semifinalists "spin their yarns."

While a second notice will outline the rules for the contest in greater detail, I would like you to have a general idea of what is expected.

- The story (folk tale, fairy tale, fable) must be memorized.
- The story must not take longer than two minutes to tell.
- The use of props will <u>not</u> be permitted.
- Criteria for judging will include: use of voice, expression, eye contact, timing, enunciation, and poise.

Ms. Tindell, our school librarian, has a collection of stories suitable for telling, as does the Southwood Public Library. School readers and books at home are other good sources of stories to memorize.

There are two city-wide categories:

Level I –Third and Fourth Graders and

Level II–Fifth and Sixth Graders

More details will follow. Mr. Corbett and Mrs. Morris will judge the contest.

V. DiAngelo, Principal

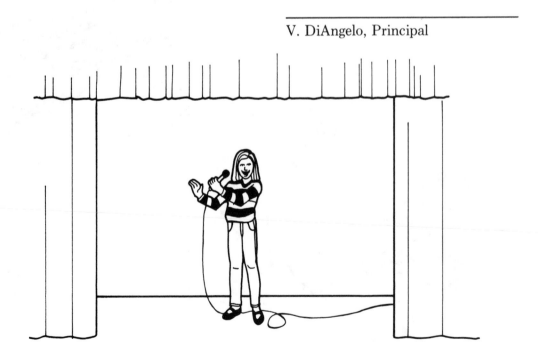

Letter 5–34: WATER-SAVING REPORT CARD

REPORT TO PARENTS
GRADES 2–7

Name of Pupil: _____

Date: _____

The purpose of this report is to have you join your child and our school in a campaign to save water. At assemblies and in classrooms we have urged our pupils to stop wasting water. We want every child to report to his or her parent any leaks or other wasteful practice.

This project offers you another opportunity to cooperate with your child and the school in working toward a common goal. Please assist your "leak seeker" by completing this Report Card together.

RATINGS USED
E = Excellent   G = Good   F = Fair   U = Unsatisfactory

	E G F U		E G F U
DRIPS		**CLEANLINESS**	
Shuts off water promptly.	— — — —	Keeps clothing clean.	— — — —
Replaces washers.	— — — —		
		PETS	— — — —
DRINKING	— — — —	Keep pets from wasting	
Keeps water in refrigerator.	— — — —	water.	— — — —
Does not let water run.	— — — —	Uses dry shampoo.	— — — —
HYGIENE	— — — —	**PLANTS**	— — — —
Takes short showers.	— — — —	Uses "recycled" clear cook-	
Bathes in half-filled tub.	— — — —	ing water.	— — — —
Shaves with water in sink.	— — — —	Keeps water from running	
Brushes teeth using a single		out of bottoms of plants.	— — — —
glass of water.	— — — —		
		CARS AND BIKES	— — — —
FLUSHING	— — — —	Uses "recycled" water to	
Does not dump cigarettes in		wash vehicles.	— — — —
the toilet bowl.	— — — —		
Flushes only when neces-		**COMMUNICATION**	— — — —
sary.	— — — —	Makes others aware of	
Listens for any tank leaks.	— — — —	water conservation.	— — — —
WASHING	— — — —	**HYDRANTS**	— — — —
Uses the dishwasher only		Reports leaking fire hy-	
when there is a full load.	— — — —	drants to the Public Works	
Washes dishes in a pan.	— — — —	Department.	— — — —
Washes clothes only when			
there is a full load.	— — — —		

Letter 5–35: WOMEN'S HISTORY WEEK

Dear Friend and Neighbor,

Mother's Day was created, originally, to honor the many contributions women make to the lives of their children and families. Today we recognize that the contributions of women extend far beyond the realm of the family, into every aspect of modern life, and into the history of our nation.

Women's History Week is an observance that picks up where Mother's Day leaves off. It is a time for honoring the contributions of all the women who have come before us, and those who are, today, creating a better world.

Our school has started a new tradition for Mother's Day, linking the lives of the women close to us with the whole of women's history. We are honoring two women from our community with a "Women of Achievement" award in our auditorium on May 3 at 11 o'clock. This year we are honoring Paula Fisher and Carolyn Angelica.

Please honor us and our Women of Achievement by attending. Husbands and others are most welcome. If you have any questions, please call me at 761-5511.

Sincerely,

_____

V. DiAngelo, Principal

SECTION
6

Letters
to
The Community

Letter 6–1: ALUMNI ASSOCIATION

TO: Graduates of P.S. 54

I would like to invite each of you to attend our Alumni Association Meeting on March 9, 19XX.

We will be meeting at a dinner dance on March 9th at 8:00 P.M. in our new gymnasium. Tickets will be available at the door at $10 each. A flyer is attached giving details.

Doesn't it seem like just a few years ago when you started at P.S. 54? Can you remember back to your very first day of school? Did it seem that it would take forever for you to become like those "big guys" in eighth grade? When you became an eighth grader, didn't it seem as if it would be forever before you graduated from high school?

If you are like the rest of us, that is exactly the way it was. Yet, somehow, those days passed (all too quickly according to some) and here you are, graduated from our school, busy with your adult life, and reading this alumni bulletin.

It is my sincere hope that what you will read here will allow you to pause for a moment and reflect on the days you spent in our school. I hope that in those reflections you will smile a bit as you recall those days of youth. I hope you will return to your school for a while and savor the time you spent there.

I'll see you on March 9th.

Sincerely,

_____

V. DiAngelo, Principal

Letter 6–2: ALUMNI FUND RAISING

TO: Former Pupils of P.S. 54
RE: Alumni Fund Raising

It has been a while since you received our end-of-year status report. In it I described some of the exciting new programs we have put in place at your "old" school.

While we are a tax-supported institution, many of our special programs such as computer education and Art-in-the-School Project have been supported by private donations.

We are now faced with budget cuts that have doomed our extracurricular program. If you think back to afternoons spent happily at dances, field trips, sports, and games, you know how important after school programs are.

If you are one of those pupils who can recall the wide offering of extracurricular activities at P.S. 54, you will know what to do. The enclosed envelope and description of prizes are self-explanatory.

Thank you,

_____

V. DiAngelo, Principal

Letter 6–3: BOOK FAIR

Dear Parent:

Would you like to give your child an entertaining, educational gift that can last a lifetime and cost $2.00? You can by helping your child select a book at our School Book Fair. We will be offering current best-sellers for children: classic favorites and new titles. Prices range from $2.00 to $3.50 for books!

You have probably spent more than that on batteries for a soon forgotten toy. These library-approved, color-illustrated, paper-covered books are publisher's close-outs. You can spark your child's interest in reading with the best in children's books at prices 50 percent to 75 percent off the hard-cover retail price.

In addition to providing our pupils with discounted books:

- <u>Every</u> pupil coming to the Book Fair in Grades K through 2 will receive a plastic book mark—even if he/she doesn't buy a book.

- <u>Every</u> pupil in Grades 3 through 5 will have a chance to win a pair of book ends just for visiting the Book Fair.

- Our school will receive dictionaries and other reference books for classroom use as a result of the Book Fair.

REMEMBER THE DATE: Thursday, March 17, in the Auditorium.

Classes will visit according to this schedule:

Parents are encouraged to come at <u>any</u> of these times:

	In Front	In Rear
9:30–10:00	K1-207, K2-116, K3-211	5-318, 5-317
10:00–10:30	K4-205, K5-213, K6-212	5-319, 5-320
10:30–11:00	K7-113, 1-215, 1-119	4-307, 4-314
11:00–11:30	1-218, 1-214, 1-216	4-117, 4-309
1:00– 1:30	2-120, 2-217	3-305, 3-312
1:30– 2:00	2-118, 2-219	3-220

Yours truly,

_____

V. DiAngelo, Principal

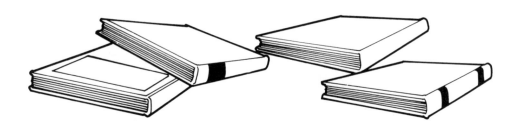

Letter 6–4: BOOSTER AD

BOOSTER AD

I am interested in placing an advertisement in the P.S. 54 Yearbook. Enclosed is my check for $ _____.

Full Page =

Half Page =

Quarter Page =

One-line Booster =

_____ I prefer that you photocopy my business card which is enclosed.

_____ Please print the following message:

_____
Signature

Letter 6–5: COMMUNITY EVALUATION QUESTIONNAIRE

TO: School Volunteers
RE: Evaluation Questionnaire

We appreciate your help this year as a school/community volunteer. The many hours of service you provided our school or our community helped our pupils grow and develop. It is my sincere wish that you continue again next year. In order to help us plan ahead and evaluate our program we ask that you take a few minutes now to respond to these questions. You may write on the back or on additional sheets if you wish. You may sign this questionnaire if you wish.

Again, thank you.

1. Do you plan to volunteer again next year?
2. What part of the program was most meaningful for you?
3. Can you recommend any changes?
4. What was the attitude of the staff?
5. How would you characterize the response of the children?
6. Were your talents and interests utilized?
7. What would you like to do next year, if you return?
8. What do you see as the greatest need for volunteers at our school?
9. How can this need be met?
10. Do you wish to recommend anyone to us as a prospective volunteer?

Letter 6–6: COMMUNITY VOLUNTEERS

A CALL FOR KINDERGARTEN HELPERS!

Again this year we are seeking the help of volunteers in our Kindergarten classrooms. Please look at this list of items. If this kind of program interests you, please fill in the coupon at the bottom and return it to the school.

DUTIES

1. Helping to arrange the physical setup of the classroom.
2. Preparing materials; setting out paints, paper supplies, dolls, blocks, and other play and educational equipment.
3. Mounting displays, making posters, arranging the bulletin board.
4. Helping with classroom decorations for special holidays and parties.
5. Assisting teachers on trips and visits outside of the classroom.
6. Helping at snack time with milk and cookies.
7. Assisting in the physical needs of children such as going to the bathroom, helping them with outer clothing, washing up.
8. Reading or storytelling.
9. Playing the piano or other musical instruments for singing, rhythms, or musical games.
10. Working on a one-to-one relationship with individual children who are not ready for group activity.
11. Helping children who do not speak English to build vocabulary.
12. Accompanying the teachers on home visits when requested.
13. Helping teachers supervise children during outdoor play.
14. Doing clerical jobs of various kinds.

Dear _____,

I am interested in working in the Kindergarten Volunteer Program. My name

is _____ and I can be reached at _____ during

the hours of _____.

I am interested in the following duties:

_____

_____

_____
Signature

Letter 6–7: COOKIE SALE

TO: All Parents

Beginning Monday, February 5, 19XX, our school will sell cookies and brownies to pupils in the lunchroom after the pupils have eaten their lunch. The cookies and brownies will cost 25 cents per individual package. The proceeds will go toward the Senior Class Trip to Metro Fun Park in June.

A committee of parents and teachers surveyed several vendors. We selected the Sugar Bear Cookie Company because we felt that they offered a wholesome product at a fair price. The purchase of these items is entirely voluntary. After your child has had a chance to sample the items, I would appreciate hearing your comments. We will have a display at the next P.T.A. meeting, where you will be welcome to taste these treats.

Sincerely,

_____

V. DiAngelo, Principal

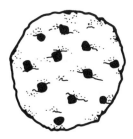  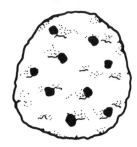

Letter 6–8: COVER LETTER FOR APPLICATIONS TO FOUNDATIONS/CORPORATIONS

Type of Support Requested: _____
(Grant, Contract, Fellowship, Scholarship)

1. Submitted to: _____

   Address with ZIP Code: _____

   _____

2. Proposed Project:

   Title: _____

   From: _____ To: _____

   Amount Requested: _____

3. Submitted by: _____
   (Name of Applicant Organization)

   Address with ZIP Code: _____

   _____

   Type of Institution:

   A. Profit ____ Nonprofit ____ Commercial _____

   B. Federal ____ State ____ Local _____ Other _____

4. Principal Investigator or _____

   Project Director (or both): _____

   Address with ZIP Code: _____

   _____

   _____   _____
   (Social Security No.)   (Telephone with Area Code)

5. Human Subjects Involved: No _____ Yes _____

Approved: _____
(Date)

Pending Approval: _____
(Date)

6. Project Site: _____

_____

7. Fiscal Agent: _____

_____

8. Endorsements:

Principal Investigator _____ _____
(Signature)   (Typed/Printed Name)

Approving Institutional _____ _____
Official   (Signature)   (Typed/Printed Name)

Other Approving _____ _____
Official   (Signature)   (Typed/Printed Name)

9. Date Submitted _____

Letter 6–9: COVER LETTER FOR APPLICATIONS TO GOVERNMENT AGENCIES

Type of Support Requested: _____

1. Submitted to: _____

   Address with ZIP Code: _____

   _____

2. Proposed Project:

   Title _____

   From: _____ To: _____

   Amount Requested: _____   _____
                  (Total)   (First 12 Months)

   _____   _____
   Overhead/Indirect Cost   Overhead/Indirect Cost (first 12 Months)

3. Submitted by: _____
                  (Name of Applicant Organization)

   Address with ZIP Code: _____

   _____

   Type of Institution:

         A. Profit ____ Nonprofit ____ Commercial _____

         B. Federal ____ State ____ Local ____ Other _____

   IRS Identification Number: _____ Congressional District_____

   Identity No. _____ Civil Rights Compliance Filed _____
                                            (date)

4. Principal Investigator or _____

   Project Director (or Both): _____

   Address with ZIP Code: _____

   _____

5. Human Subjects Involved: No _____ Yes _____

Approved: _____

Pending Approval: _____

6. Indicate if proposal has been or will be submitted in whole or in part to other possible sponsors, including other governmental agencies, and name the agencies: _____

_____

7. Project Site: _____

_____

8. Fiscal Agent: _____

_____

9. Endorsements
   Principal Investigator _____ _____
                          (Signature)   (Typed/Printed Name)
   Approving Institutional
      Official   _____ _____
                          (Signature)   (Typed/Printed Name)

   Other Approving _____ _____
      Official   (Signature)   (Typed/Printed Name)

10. Date Submitted _____

Letter 6–10: KINDERGARTEN REGISTRATION

March, 19XX

Dear Parents:

During the period of April 28 through May 16, children will be registered for Kindergarten and for the first grade. Children who are currently in Kindergarten do not have to be registered.

Children born during the calendar year 19_____ are eligible to enter Kindergarten in September, 19_____. Children born in 19_____ are eligible to enter first grade. Please bring this notice to the attention of neighbors whose children fall within these age groups.

Important Instructions for Registration

1. The child to be registered <u>must</u> be present.
2. The parent must bring the following:
   a. Birth Certificate (or a baptismal certificate) properly signed by an authorized official with an accompanying seal on the certificate.
   b. Proof of immunizations including polio, measles, rubella, mumps, and diptheria.
   c. Proof of address (utility bill).
3. Every child entering school is required by the Health Code to have a medical examination. This may be done after registration by the family physician, by a clinic physician of a child health station of the Department of Health, or by a school physician.
4. At the time of registration, the parent will fill out a self-addressed postal card. Several days before the opening of school on September 5, these cards will be mailed to parents, indicating class placement.
5. If, subsequently, the parent finds it necessary to cancel this registration, it is his responsibility to notify the school in writing.
6. Any children registered in Kindergarten during this period who do not appear by the Wednesday following the opening of school in September will be placed on a waiting list unless the school has been notified of the child's inability to attend, and the reason is a valid one. Children with <u>incomplete</u> medical records—see Item 2b—will also be put on a waiting list.

Very truly yours,

_____

V. DiAngelo, Principal

Letter 6–11: MINI MARATHON

TO: All Boys and Girls

We are going to hold a Mini Marathon to benefit the Library Fund. It will be held on Thursday, April 26, 19XX at 10 o'clock. The starting point is our schoolyard fence.

Ask your family and friends to sponsor you. They will be asked to contribute $1.00 for every mile you run. If you run a half-mile they will be asked to contribute a half-dollar. The complete distance is three miles, so if you complete the Mini Marathon, they will contribute a maximum of $3.00.

Follow these simple rules:

1. Fill out the registration card.

2. Sign up sponsors. (See below.)

3. Encourage friends and family to walk, too.

4. Bring both copies of your sponsor sheet with you to the Mini Marathon.

5. After the Mini Marathon, collect your sponsors' contributions.

6. Bring your contributions to the school office on Monday, April 30, 19XX.

Good luck!

SPONSOR SHEET

	Name	Address	Pledge/Mile(s)
1.			
2.			
3.			
4.			
5.			
6.			
7.			
8.			
9.			
10.			
11.			

(Use another sheet if you need more space for sponsors.)

Letter 6-12: NURSING HOME VISIT

TO: Parents of Pupils in the Band
RE: Visit to Golden Age Nursing Home

   In addition to acquiring a solid foundation in basic skills, our pupils are learning a great deal about life in our modern world. Among other things, we are trying to foster an understanding of the dignity and worth of every individual in our society.

   One aspect of this program is an appreciation of the contributions of members of earlier generations. Our pupils are sharing their love of music with the senior citizens at the Golden Age Nursing Home on March 18, 19XX. At that time, our band pupils will perform in the Golden Age Auditorium at 10:30 A.M. Following their instrumental selections, members of the Golden Age Chorus will sing a medley of songs for our pupils.

   We hope that this exchange of talent will give our band students a better understanding and a deeper respect for our aging population. You are most welcome to join us on March 18. Just call my office to ensure a seat on the bus.

                                        Sincerely,

                                        _____

                                        V. DiAngelo, Principal

Letter 6–13: NURSERY SCHOOL VISIT

Dear Mrs. Merzinski:

I am writing this letter of invitation to you in your capacity as Director of a nursery school in our community. We at P.S. 54 have, in the past, received many pupils who spent a year or more at your nursery school. Our Kindergarten and First Grade teachers have found them to be well prepared and self-confident after completing your program.

We would like to have you visit our school on February 16 to see our Early Childhood grades in action and meet our teachers. Such direct communication will prove to be mutually beneficial. We would welcome a visit of your pupils to our school in the spring. We will have a tour of the Kindergarten rooms and a snack in the lunchroom.

Please let me know if this date is convenient. I look forward to seeing you.

Sincerely,

_____

V. DiAngelo, Principal

Letter 6-14: PLANT SALE

May 1, 19XX

Dear Students, Parents, Teachers, and Staff:

Hi, it's that time of year again!

Spring is in the air, and what can be more beautiful than giving someone you love a beautiful plant? So, let's think about Mother's Day.

Our Plant Sale is being held on Friday, May 8, 19XX.

We will have a large variety of plants and vegetables to sell:

Flowers	Hanging Baskets
wax begonias	wax begonias
coleus	impatiens
petunias	petunias
impatiens	
marigolds	
dusty miller	Vegetables
croton gold dust	
African violets	tomatoes
geraniums	green peppers
	eggplant

Our plants will range in price from $.50 to $2.50.

We will also have a bargain table available.

Please be sure to bring a paper bag for your purchases.

See you all at the sale.

_____

V. DiAngelo, Principal

Letter 6–15: READING VOLUNTEERS

Dear Friends:

Do you enjoy reading? Do you like spending time with young people? We have a wonderful opportunity for you at P.S. 54. We need Reading Volunteers to come into school two days a week to spend two hours reading with some of our pupils. The hours are flexible and the rewards are boundless.

We will hold a training session the week of October 8, 19XX. At that time you will be shown specific techniques, and receive reading materials and grade level assignments. Please fill out this short survey form and drop it off at the school or mail it.

I look forward to welcoming you on October 8, 19XX, at 10 o'clock in the school lunchroom.

Cordially,

_____

V. DiAngelo, Principal

Name: _____   Phone: _____

Address: _____

Age Level Preferred: _____

Which activity appeals to you the most?

_____ Reading aloud to a small group

_____ Reading along with a pupil requiring reading help

_____ Math tutoring   _____ Library aide

Days willing to work (list two)

Hours willing to work (list two-hour span)

Letter 6–16:   REZONING

TO: Residents of our School Community
RE: Rezoning of P.S. 54
FR: V. DiAngelo, Principal

As members of our school community, I'm sure you share my concerns about the plans for rezoning our school. Please come to this very important meeting. We need your input.

The public meeting in this year's annual review of the rezoning plan has been scheduled as follows:

Tuesday, December 16—Susan B. Anthony H.S. Auditorium
3:00 to 5:00 P.M. and 7:00 to 9:00 P.M.

The first half hour of each session will be used to explain the tentative proposal. A copy of this proposal was mailed early in November. This proposal was developed within the guidelines of the objectives discussed at the first meeting, after a careful study of the diverse input from the above groups.

I invite you to share with us your concerns and comments on the proposal. Additional copies will be available at the meeting. If you would like us to give you an additional copy before the meeting, please stop by the District Office. Since the purpose of this meeting is to hear and record your ideas and feelings, you will be able to arrange for speaking time when you arrive. You need not, therefore, make prior arrangements for speaking time.

If you are not able to join us, and if you have not already done so, you may send us your written suggestions before December 16. Please write "P.S. 54 Zoning" on your envelope to expedite its handling and study. We will then prepare a proposed plan, reflecting all input, which will be presented to Superintendent Woodbury. His zoning plan will be issued as soon as possible thereafter.

Letter 6–17: SCHOOL PICTURES

TO: All Parents

On Thursday, October 25, 19XX, the school photographer will be here to photograph our pupils. This is our big fund raiser of the year. Last year's proceeds paid for our new VCR in the Library and for science materials for the third grade.

Class pictures will be taken, as well as individual poses. A brochure giving the cost of each package is enclosed.

Please make sure your child is wearing a light-colored shirt or top on October 25. Volunteer parents will be present to comb their hair when needed. We hope to get the photos back for distribution in five weeks. Please make checks payable to Tru-Image Inc.

Your child's class will be photographed at _____ o'clock. If you wish to bring a preschool child to be photographed, you may do so in the Auditorium at 2:00 P.M.

Thank you,

_____

V. DiAngelo, Principal

Letter 6–18: SPECIAL OLYMPICS

TO: News Editor of TV or Radio Station
RE: Request for Coverage

On Saturday May 16, 19XX, from 1:00 P.M. to 3:00 P.M. at P.S. 54, special Olympic games will be played. Over 100 handicapped and special education children will participate in modified track and field events in the Athletic Field behind the school.

These children, between the ages of 6 and 14, will compete in races and other events under the leadership of the Special Education Department of the County Community College. Dr. Harry Gilburt, Chairman of Health and Physical Education is Co-chairman of the Special Olympics along with Mrs. Cathy Edwards, President of the school P.T.A.

This is the first time that our blind and hard-of-hearing pupils will be included in the events. More than 300 parents and friends will attend.

Additional information can be obtained from:

V. DiAngelo
Principal, P.S. 54
761-5511

Dr. Harry Gilburt
Community College
345-3456

Mrs. Cathy Edwards
P.T.A. President
456-7879

Letter 6–19: SPRING CONCERT

TO: All Band Parents
FR: V. DiAngelo, Principal
RE: Spring Concert

      On Wednesday, May 15th, at 7:30 P.M., the 4th and 5th graders will be performing in our annual spring concert.

      We would appreciate it very much if you could donate a cake for our cake sale which will be held before and after the concert. The cakes should be brought to P.S. 54 from 6:30 to 7:00 P.M. The proceeds from the sale will be used for maintenance and repair of instruments. Your support is very much appreciated.

      I hope to see you and your family on May 15th.

Letter 6–20: VOLUNTEER PROGRAM

TO: Community Residents
FR: V. DiAngelo, Principal

      The purpose of the Volunteer Program is to provide an opportunity for parents and other interested adults to assist school personnel in the operation of the schools. Such services are valuable in library work, hot lunch programs, aiding teachers within the classrooms, and assisting in the administrative offices. Contact the office to volunteer.

      The Parent-Teacher Association of P.S. 54 is coordinating the Volunteer Program. If you can help in any of the areas listed below, please indicate your interests. Please consider participating in some way. We appreciate your help.

1. Dance Chaperones
2. Library
3. Nurse's Office (Two hours per week doing typing and/or clerical work)
4. Lunch Program
5. Telephoning and Office Help
6. Classroom Work
7. Other (suggestions sought)

NAME _____

TELEPHONE _____

GRADE OF CHILD IN SCHOOL (if you have one) _____

COMMENTS _____

_____

_____

_____

Letter 6–21: VOLUNTEER TUTORS

TO: Volunteer Tutors
FR: V. DiAngelo, Principal
RE: Evaluation Form

We are most grateful for your help this year as a volunteer tutor. Please take a few moments to answer these questions. Your reply will be helpful to next year's tutors. Again, thank you. (Use the back of this sheet to answer the questions.)

1. List the most important things you did as a tutor.
2. How much do tutors help a class?

   _____ Very helpful   _____ Some help   _____ No help

3. Did you help students and teachers understand each other and get along better together?

   _____ Very helpful   _____ Some help   _____ No help

4. What percent of your tutoring time did you spend with:

   _____ Individuals?   _____ Small groups?   _____ Whole Class?

5. Do most students seem to welcome or resent the use of tutors?

   _____ Welcome   _____ Resent

6. Give an example of how you helped one student.
7. Give an example of how you helped a small group or a whole class.
8. In selecting tutors, what characteristics (kind of person) should be looked for?
   (List the most important characteristics first.)
9. Who should evaluate the tutors' work.?
10. How should the tutor be evaluated?
11. Should orientation meetings be held before classes are assigned?

    _____ Yes   _____ No

12. Should all the tutors and all the teachers using tutors meet as a large group now and then?

    _____ Yes   _____ No   _____ How often?   _____ Why?

13. How much has the tutor seminar helped you to be a better tutor?

    _____ Very helpful   _____ Some help   _____ No help

14. Has your work as a tutor been helpful to you?

    _____ Very helpful   _____ Some help   _____ No help
    Explain your answer.

Letter 6–22: WRITING PRESS RELEASES

TO: Teachers
FR: V. DiAngelo, Principal
RE: Writing Press Releases

Many of your classroom and after-school activities are worthy of a story in the daily newspaper or a segment on the local TV news.

Neither Channel 3 nor the <u>Daily Record</u> will publicize your activities unless they get a suitable story outline. Please look at this checklist to see if your story idea is worthy of consideration. We in the office will be happy to polish it up for you if you give us the data.

1. Is your story idea unusual in some way? Highlight the aspects that make it unique. Think of the audience the paper or station is trying to reach.

2. Is your story upbeat and positive in tone? The stories of violence and vandalism find their way into the media without our help.

3. Does your story involve groups or individuals outside of our school? Editors like items involving parents, community members, pets, politicians, others interacting with school children.

4. Would readers or viewers other than the parents of your pupils want to read or view these items?

5. Can you find some humorous or sentimental quality to attach to your story idea?

6. Have you checked all the facts, times, dates, names and quotes for accuracy? Does your release answer the questions: who, when, what, why, and when?

7. Can the average reader or viewer identify with your story?

8. Do you have any black and white photographs to send along with the press release? Do you want to request a photographer for a later date?

9. Can you describe everything on a single typwritten page?

10. Is there a seasonal nature to your story? Are you giving the media enough lead time?